7/04

you can RENEW this item from
home by visiting our Website at
www.woodbridge.lioninc.org or by
calling (203) 389-3433

Life & Times in 20th-Century America

Volume 3: Hot and Cold Wars

1941–1960

Greenwood Publishing Group

Library of Congress Cataloging-in-Publication Data
Life & times in 20th-century America / by Media Projects, Inc.
    p. cm
    Includes bibliographical references and indexes.
  Contents: v. 1. Becoming a modern nation, 1900-1920 — v. 2. Boom times, hard times,
1921-1940 — v. 3. Hot and cold wars, 1941-1960 — v. 4. Troubled times at home,
1961-1980 — v. 5. Promise and change, 1981-2000.
ISBN 0–313–32570–7 (set: alk. paper)—ISBN 0–313–32571–5 (v. 1: alk. paper) —
ISBN 0–313–32572–3 (v. 2: alk. paper)—ISBN 0–313–32573–1 (v. 3: alk. paper) —
ISBN 0–313–32574–X (v. 4: alk. paper)—ISBN 0–313–32575–8 (v. 5: alk. paper)
  1. United States—History—20th century. 2. United States—Social conditions—20th
century. 3. United States—Social life and customs—20th century. I. Media Projects
Incorporated.
E741.L497 2004
973.91—dc21   2003044829

British Library Cataloguing in Publication Data is available.

Library of Congress Catalog Card Number: 2003044829
ISBN: 0–313–32570–7 (set)
       0–313–32571–5 (vol. 1)
       0–313–32572–3 (vol. 2)
       0–313–32573–1 (vol. 3)
       0–313–32574–X (vol. 4)
       0–313–32575–8 (vol. 5)

First published in 2004

Greenwood Press, 88 Post Road West, Westport, CT 06881
An imprint of Greenwood Publishing Group, Inc.
www.greenwood.com

Printed in the United States of America

The paper used in this book complies with the
Permanent Paper Standard issued by the National
Information Standards Organization (Z39.48–1984).

10 9 8 7 6 5 4 3 2 1

Media Projects, Inc.
Managing Editor: Carter Smith
Writer: Stuart Murray
Editor: Carolyn Jackson
Production Editor: Jim Burmester
Indexer: Marilyn Flaig
Designer: Amy Henderson
Copy Editor: Elin Woodger

Contents

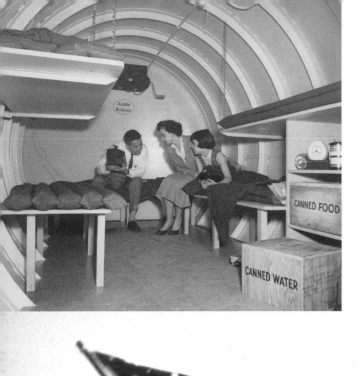

Victory, Prosperity, and Cold War

In the first months of 1940, Americans watched uneasily as the European powers prepared for yet another conflict. This one promised to be worse than the Great War (1914–1918), which would soon be renamed World War I.

The more than 3,000 miles of Atlantic Ocean between the United States and Europe seemed a safeguard, but no one knew what the future would hold. Germany had assembled powerful armies along its frontier with France and the Lowland Countries of Holland, Belgium, and Luxembourg. Facing the Germans were the French and British forces, also massed for war. Who would strike first?

The democracies of Great Britain and France had declared war on Germany because it had invaded Poland the year before. Germany was under the dictatorship of Adolf Hitler and his National Socialist political party—called Nazis. Nazi policy proclaimed a "master race" in which Jews and other "undesirables" had no right to life or property. At the same time, Hitler claimed the right to rule all those regions where people of German ancestry lived. One such region was part of Poland, taken from Germany after its defeat in the Great War. In the 1939 invasion, Germany retook this region from Poland. Now the British and French were determined to force Germany to withdraw. War seemed unavoidable.

The people of the United States debated whether to stay out of the conflict or to take sides with Britain and France. At that time, the U.S. Army was only seventeenth in the world in size. The United States, like Europe, was just coming out of the Great Depression. That decade-long economic crisis had demanded extraordinary efforts from President Franklin D. Roosevelt and the U.S. Congress.

CLOCKWISE: **A family in their backyard bomb shelter; Elvis Presley; U.S. troops raise the flag at Okinawa, during World War II.** (All photos: Library of Congress)

First elected in 1932, Roosevelt had promoted new federal programs designed to help the unemployed by creating public-works projects that gave jobs to millions of Americans. This economic recovery plan was known as the New Deal, meaning it gave people a better opportunity, a fresh start, like a new deal from a deck of cards.

Now Roosevelt was about to run for a third four-year term. No other president had ever held office more than two terms. Roosevelt was a Democrat and a former governor of New York State. He promised, if reelected, to continue the policies of his New Deal program. This involved the federal government in solving social problems more than ever before. He had persuaded Congress to pass laws to help farmers and to regulate banking and investing. He had also helped put people to work building dams, bridges, roads, and public housing. For the first time, the U.S. government guaranteed regular assistance to the old, disabled, and sick through Social Security.

Roosevelt also promised to keep the country out of war, as did his Republican opponent Wendell L. Willkie.

Lightning War

In May 1940, Nazi forces suddenly launched an offensive against the British and French.

In a few weeks of *blitzkrieg*, or "lightning war," hard-hitting German ground troops and tanks, supported by airplanes, rolled through the

1940

Germany invades Belgium, the Netherlands, and France. In July, it launches the Battle of Britain, the first wave of a planned sea invasion of the British Isles. When the British win control of the skies, the German plan for invasion is halted.

1940

For the first time in its history, the U.S. government orders a military draft while the nation is at peace.

1941

Democrat Franklin D. Roosevelt is inugurated for his third term after defeating Republican Wendell L. Willkie in the previous fall's presidential election.

1941

President Roosevelt signs the Lend-Lease Act. The law allows him to lend or lease military supplies to Britian. Hundreds of supply ships sail to Britain to help that country defend itself against Germany.

Lowland Countries. Next, France was quickly defeated and occupied. British forces that had been stationed in Europe retreated to help defend their island nation. Italy, also under a dictatorship, joined Germany in an alliance known as the Axis Powers. In Asia, Japan had built an empire that included conquered lands in Korea and much of China.

These three aggressor nations—Germany, Italy, and Japan—were all run by fascist governments. In such governments, the state controls the political and economic systems and does not allow free elections or human rights.

Germany attacked Britain by air and threatened to invade it. Roosevelt called upon the United States to become the "arsenal of democracy." Throughout 1941, it sent hundreds of ships loaded with supplies, equipment, and armaments to help Britain hold out. However, the conflict soon spread to Yugoslavia, Greece, and North Africa. The situation worsened in mid-1941, when Germany and Italy suddenly attacked the Soviet Union. (The Union of Soviet Socialist Republics, or USSR, had been created in 1922 when the communist Russian government began to pull other neighboring countries into its nation. By 1946, there would be 15 republics.)

It became clear that the final goal of the fascists was to conquer as many countries as they could and dominate the world.

Although the United States was not yet directly involved in the fighting, the country's first-ever peacetime military draft was established in 1940. This steadily built up the nation's forces. U S. industry was booming,

1941

Japan launches a surprise attack on the U.S naval base at Pearl Harbor, Hawaii. The United States enters World War II the next day.

1942

Nazi dictator Adolf Hitler orders that gas chambers be installed in concentration camps set up to hold Jews, communists, political prisoners, homosexuals, and others declared "undesirable." The purpose of the gas chambers is to murder prisoners more quickly.

1944

More than 150,000 U.S., British, and Canadian soldiers land on the coast of France. The landing begins the successful liberation of Europe from the Nazis.

1944

President Roosevelt signs the GI Bill of Rights, which authorizes education, housing, and other benefits for American soldiers when they return from war. The bill helps spark the growth of the suburbs after the war.

President Franklin Roosevelt signs the declaration of war against Japan on December 8, 1941. (National Park Service)

pulling the nation out of the Great Depression at last. Factories turned out thousands upon thousands of tanks and aircraft and tons of ammunition, guns, and assorted equipment, both for the U.S. military and for the British.

Then came the shock of December 7, 1941—a day of infamy, as Roosevelt termed it—when Japan launched a surprise air attack on the American naval base at Pearl Harbor, Hawaii. The assault destroyed much of the U.S. fleet stationed there. Japan had attacked the fleet to stop the United States from interfering with its plans for conquest in the Pacific.

Within hours, the United States declared war on Japan, which had become an ally of the German-Italian Axis. Americans were now unified in their determination to fight in a conflict that could truly be called World War II.

1945

Five months after winning reelection for a fourth term as president, Franklin D. Roosevelt dies. Vice President Harry S Truman becomes president.

1945

Representatives of fifty countries meet in San Francisco to organize the United Nations. The organization will later name New York City as its headquarters.

1945

Following Hitler's suicide, Germany surrenders, ending World War II in Europe. Germany will be split in half, with the eastern half occupied by the Soviet Union and the western half governed by the United States, Great Britain, and France.

1945

The United States drops an atomic bomb on Hiroshima, Japan, killing over 138,000 people. Three days later, a second bomb is dropped, this time on the Japanese city of Nagasaki. Five days later, Japan surrenders. World War II is over.

The Nation at War

Warfare raged around the globe. On one side were the Allies: the United States, the Soviet Union, China, Great Britain, and British Commonwealth countries including Canada, Australia, New Zealand, South Africa, and India. (The British Commonwealth was made up of British colonies and former colonies that considered the British king their ruler.) On the other side were the Axis Powers: Germany, Italy, and Japan, joined by a few smaller countries.

As the war progressed, the United States became the most powerful of the Allies. It put more than 16 million men and women into uniform and built the world's strongest navy and air force. Just as important as U.S. fighting ability was its tremendous industrial output. The United States was the main source of arms and supplies for the Allies. Factories went into activity round the clock. There was employment for all, including married women, who before this time had not entered the workforce in large numbers.

The war gradually turned in favor of the Allies. By the spring of 1945, Italy had surrendered. Germany was being overwhelmed by Americans and British from the west and Russians from the east. It finally surrendered in May. America's joy at the victory was mixed with sadness, however. President Roosevelt had died in April of a cerebral hemorrhage (rupture of a blood vessel in his brain). Roosevelt's death especially saddened those who had supported his policies and respected his leadership.

1947
Jackie Robinson joins the Brooklyn Dodgers baseball team, becoming the first African American to play major-league baseball.

1948
Democrat Harry S Truman is reelected president, defeating Republican Thomas E. Dewey.

1949
The Soviet Union, or USSR, carries out its first atomic bomb test.

1950
Forces from communist North Korea invade South Korea, beginning the Korean War. In response, the United States leads a United Nations force to try to turn back the invasion. The fighting lasts for three years and ends in a draw.

Vice President Harry S Truman stepped in as the 33rd president and led the nation to final victory. This meant turning all military might against Japan as fighting continued in the Pacific. In the summer of 1945, Truman ordered atomic bombs dropped on the Japanese cities of Hiroshima and Nagasaki. More than 220,000 people were killed or

President Harry Truman (Library of Congress)

wounded by these two bombs. Hundreds of thousands more suffered from radiation poisoning from the bombs' nuclear reactions.

The Allies believed the threat of more atomic bombs would force Japan to surrender, thus preventing even greater loss of life in a full-scale Allied invasion. On August 14, 1945, immediately after the destruction of Nagasaki, Japan surrendered unconditionally. World War II had ended.

Postwar Prosperity

Fifteen million soldiers died in World War II. Approximately the same number of civilians died, either in the fighting itself, or as a result of Adolf Hitler's policies. Six million Jews, most of Europe's Jewish population, were put to death in what became known as the Holocaust. In his efforts

1950

In a speech, Senator Joseph McCarthy of Wisconsin accuses the U.S. State Department of employing 205 communists. For the next four years, McCarthy will lead investigations into communist spying in the United States.

1952

General Dwight D. Eisenhower, a Republican, wins the presidential election of 1952, defeating Senator Adlai Stevenson, a Democrat.

1954

The Supreme Court rules in the case of *Brown v. Board of Education of Topeka (Kansas)* that racial segregation in public schools is unconstitutional.

1954

Elvis Presley begins recording for Sun Records. He quickly becomes the nation's leading recording star and helps to popularize rock and roll music.

to create a "pure" race, Hitler had killed millions of gypsies, Slavs, homosexuals and others deemed opponents of the state.

U.S. casualties numbered more than 405,000 dead, with 670,846 wounded. Such losses caused deep sorrow to the nation.

At the same time, the war effort brought great national prosperity. Between 1939 and the end of the war in 1945, American factories almost doubled their production. The economy boomed, and Americans continued to move from one place to another. The population was shifting steadily westward. In California, new communities grew up around major manufacturing regions.

At the war's end, millions of couples began to have children. From the mid-1940s to 1950, more than 30 million children were born. The sudden rise in births was called a baby boom, and the children were later called baby boomers.

Government loan programs made it possible for many ex-servicemen to go to college and for young families to buy new homes. These programs were established under an act of Congress called the GI Bill, named after the slang term for a U.S. soldier that meant "government issue."

Cold War Conflicts

World War II made the United States the world leader militarily and economically. Yet victory did not begin an era of world peace. America's

1955

Rosa Parks, an African American, refuses to give up her seat to a white man and is arrested. The African American community in Montgomery, Alabama, led by the Reverend Martin Luther King, Jr., begins a boycott of local buses.

1957

The Soviet Union launches *Sputnik*, the first artificial satellite, into outer space.

1959

Alaska and Hawaii enter the union as the forty-ninth and fiftieth states in the United States.

1960

Senator John F. Kennedy, a Democrat, defeats Vice President Richard M. Nixon, a Republican, in the presidential election.

former ally, the Soviet Union, was now its rival.

Ruled by the totalitarian, or all-powerful, centralized authority of the Communist Party, the Soviet Union took control of Eastern Europe after the war. It fortified this new frontier with, which Winston Churchill, the wartime British prime minister, called an Iron Curtain. This frontier divided what became known as the free world countries of Western Europe like Great Britain, France, and Allied-occupied West Germany from Communist-dominated countries like Hungary, Czechoslovakia, Poland, Romania, and the newly created East Germany. The old German capital of Berlin, inside East Germany, was divided into four parts. Those held by France, Great Britain, and the United States became part of West Berlin. The Soviets installed a communist government in their part of East Berlin.

A new international conflict began between the Soviet Union and the United States and their respective allies. This was not a "hot war" in which the two main powers blasted away at each other. Instead, it was a "cold war" of ideas, between types of governments (free democracies and communist dictatorships) and between economic systems (free-market capitalism and state-controlled socialism). Each superpower, as the United States and Soviet Union were sometimes called, sought to win other nations to its side. When armed conflict broke out, it did not spread across the world.

Yet the Cold War threatened humankind's annihilation. The Soviet Union had obtained its first atomic weapon in 1949. Now East and West aimed thousands of nuclear weapons at each another. There was now the fear that some political spark might unleash "the Bomb" and that nuclear warfare resulting in devastation and radiation poisoning would make the world not fit to live in.

The Cold War was a standoff between democratic capitalism and totalitarian communism. Soviet communism developed from the teachings of the German Karl Marx, who had observed that whoever controls wealth and property (capital) in a society controls the means of production. The People's Republic of China set up a system similar to the Soviet one after the Communist Party came to power in 1949, although the two nations were often rivals.

With some exceptions, wealth and property in the West were privately

In 1956, Hungarians rebelled against their country's domination by the Soviet Union. Citizens of Budapest, the nation's capital, are seen here on top of a Soviet tank. The Soviet Union would crush the rebellion by force—killing over 7,000 Hungarians in the process. (Hulton-Getty Images)

owned and controlled, and commerce was free. Such a capitalist system, combined with free elections, encouraged personal freedom.

President Truman's Response

The Cold War divided most of the world into two great, armed camps. President Truman's "containment policy" opposed Communist expansion. Under Truman, the Central Intelligence Agency was founded in 1947 to counter communist spying.

Truman, a Democrat from Missouri, was not popular, even with some other Democrats. Northerners who had liked Roosevelt for his social grace and wealthy background showed little enthusiasm for the unpolished Truman. Southern Democrats viewed him as too liberal when it came to racial integration. In the South, African Americans were legally segregated from whites. They were treated as second-class citizens. (There was segregation in the North too, but by custom, not law.) Truman ordered racial integration of the government's civilian workforce and the military. Before

Truman's order, the military had placed African Americans in separate units.

In international affairs, Truman supported policies that helped Western Europe rebuild after the war. From 1948 to 1952, the United States provided $12 billion in loans and financial aid that were crucial to European recovery. Truman also led in the effort to create an international organization that offered the world its greatest hope for peace: the United Nations (UN). Americans were more willing now to support a world organization than they were after World War I, when the Senate had rejected the League of Nations.

The United Nations was founded at the close of World War II in order to keep peace and promote commerce and development. The first major military contest facing the UN was the Korean War. The war began in 1950 when the communist People's Republic of North Korea invaded the non-communist Republic of South Korea. To turn back the invasion, the United States led a force of UN troops in a three-year struggle.

Communist Chinese soldiers entered this undeclared war on the side of North Korea. China shared a border with North Korea that UN troops did not cross. The fighting ended in a draw in 1953 that established a heavily fortified "line of demarcation" between North and South Korea. Perhaps a million people had died, more than 54,000 of them Americans.

A major Cold War conflict had turned "hot" but was now over. Nevertheless, U.S. troops remained in South Korea to keep the peace into the twenty-first century. Many more potentially dangerous situations were heating up all around the world.

The Red Scare

Soviet dictator Joseph Stalin was the world's leading communist figure. He labeled those who opposed him—former allies, landowners, critical scientists, writers, and artists—enemies of the state. For the slightest offense, they might be persecuted, jailed, or murdered. Such drastic retaliation against real or imagined offenses created a reign of terror. Stalin announced his intention to dominate the world. Along with concerns about the atomic bomb and communist aggression in other countries, Americans worried that communists might threaten their own government and society.

Rumors spread that thousands of undercover communist sympathizers were secretly working with Stalin's agents to weaken and destroy the democracies of the West. (This anxiety was known as the Red Scare because red was the symbolic color of international communism. Pink was used to label those sympathetic to communism but not members of the Communist Party.)

Indeed, since the 1930s, some U.S. citizens had joined the Communist Party or shared its announced goals of peace and equality. Although Stalin's actions disillusioned some of these people, they also admired the way that Russian communists had stood up to Nazi Germany. Beginning in 1950, a Senate committee headed by Joseph McCarthy investigated charges that there were communists hiding throughout the government. The Federal Bureau of Investigation (FBI) opened files on thousands of suspected Communists.

Senator Joseph McCarthy
(Library of Congress)

In time, and after much public debate, it became obvious to most that fears of secret communist agents lurking around every corner were not based in reality. By then, many innocent Americans had lost their jobs after being falsely labeled "red." The Senate finally showed its disapproval of McCarthy by censuring, or disciplining, him in 1954. However, the FBI continued its investigations of individuals into the 1970s.

The Domino Theory

In its role as policeman of the world, the United States tried to stop communism from spreading. In 1953, General Dwight D. Eisenhower succeeded Truman as president. Eisenhower, who had led Allied forces in Europe during World War II, saw neutral nations as a row of dominoes. If one nation fell to communists, he told a news conference, it would push over the nation next to it, then the next and the next.

In Vietnam, Ho Chi Minh, a local communist leader, sought to establish an independent state. Vietnam had been part of the French colony of Indochina before Japan had invaded during World War II. After the war,

France wanted to return to power there. The United States first backed the French. After they were driven out in 1954, a civil war continued between Ho Chi Minh's communist forces in the north and capitalist forces in the south. The United States supported the southern part of the nation, aiming to prevent Ho Chi Minh from coming to power. That entanglement would continue until 1973.

In the Western Hemisphere, one of the most dramatic Cold War events was the 1959 revolution in Cuba, which had been ruled by an oppressive dictator. Led by Fidel Castro, the revolution seemed like a genuinely popular uprising, a quest for more freedom. The United States did not oppose it.

Soon after his victory, however, Castro shocked America by taking over U.S.-owned sugar plantations and businesses. When the United States penalized the country for not paying the owners, Castro turned to the Soviet Union for help. Cuba, just ninety miles from the U.S. mainland, became another communist state. Thousands of Cubans who opposed Castro fled the island. Most settled in Florida.

In Washington, President Eisenhower planned an invasion of Cuba to oust Castro. That invasion would not be launched until 1961, when John F. Kennedy was in the White House. It failed, and Castro remained in power for the rest of the twentieth century.

Race Relations and Social Change

Other powerful new forces were also working to influence life at home.

Since the nation began gearing up for World War I in 1914, African Americans had been migrating by the hundreds of thousands from the South to northern and midwestern cities where there were jobs. By 1930, some 1.5 million African Americans had become a part of this Great Migration. During World War II, President Roosevelt banned racial discrimination in defense industries, and still more African Americans sought jobs outside the South. When legal segregation continued down south after the war, this migration grew again.

At the same time, government programs and private banks made it easier for middle-class white families to move to the fast-growing suburbs. Housing prices dropped in the cities and black families—considerably less prosperous than the whites that had left—moved in.

The inner cities began to suffer from poverty and overcrowding. With a shortage of tax revenue to fund services such as education and sanitation, once-excellent city schools declined, and neighborhoods crumbled. A sense of hopelessness fueled drug and alcohol abuse and went hand in hand with increased crime.

An African American man in Oklahoma drinks from a water cooler set aside for "colored people." Before the 1950s, many public facilities were segregated, or divided by race. (Library of Congress)

Yet the nation was slow to remedy racial discrimination. The Congress of Racial Equality (CORE), founded in 1943, conducted the first restaurant sit-ins to protest segregation in Chicago. Black protesters refused to leave all-white restaurants, forcing restaurant owners to lose business. That same year, the shooting of a black soldier by a white policeman triggered a riot in New York's Harlem, which had been an African American neighborhood for 25 years.

In 1947, CORE organized what it called the "Journey of Reconciliation." It was designed to test whether federal laws were being enforced against discrimination in public accommodations, such as buses and trains. Black and white CORE workers traveled together on buses throughout the upper South before finally being jailed in North Carolina for causing a disturbance. President Truman failed to win support in Congress for civil-rights legislation in 1948, the same year he integrated the armed forces by executive order.

There were notable triumphs, however. Major-league baseball was integrated when Jackie Robinson joined the Brooklyn Dodgers in 1947. An even greater victory came in 1954, when the Supreme Court unanimously ruled in the case of *Brown v. Board of Education of Topeka (Kansas)* that racial segregation in elementary and secondary public schools was unconstitutional. In response, some communities in the North moved toward full integration

Rosa Parks is fingerprinted by a police officer after her arrest. (Library of Congress)

of schools, but the South showed little willingness to obey the court. Southern state laws continued to maintain segregation not only in schools and universities but also in restaurants, at drinking fountains, and on public transportation.

Then, in 1955, Montgomery, Alabama's Rosa Parks refused to move to the back of the bus, where African Americans were required to sit if a white person wanted their seat. She was arrested, angering thousands of Montgomery blacks. Led by a young minister named Martin Luther King, Jr., Montgomery's African American community decided to boycott the city bus system. For more than a full year, virtually no black men, women, or children rode a city bus. The boycott ended only when the Supreme Court ruled that bus passengers could sit wherever they wished.

White Americans were being forced to rethink long-held ideas about race. These ideas often revealed ignorance and prejudice.

Nuclear Power

For all the dangers of nuclear warfare, the Atomic Age promised more than human destruction. The power released by the splitting of the atom was also harnessed to generate electricity.

By the 1950s, nuclear-fired power plants were being built all across the country. By 1962, there were 285 nuclear power reactors in operation in the United States. They provided electricity without burning oil or coal that spewed polluting smoke. Nuclear fuel was more efficient. It did not require mining, drilling, and endless shipments of fuel. Furthermore, nuclear generating plants were much cheaper to operate than fossil-fuel plants.

At first, pollution-free nuclear energy seemed a dream come true. However, there were nagging questions about lethal radiation produced by nuclear plants and doubts about their long-term safety. For example, what was to be done with waste from nuclear fuel after it was "spent"? This atomic waste gave off dangerous radiation for many thousands of years. Where could it be stored?

Such questions were temporarily set aside, however, and nuclear power plants continued to be built. The United States had great confidence that science, technology, and American know-how soon would solve any problems.

Baby Boomers and the Suburbs

The children of the World War II generation were becoming teenagers by 1959. They had grown up in a world of goods like automobiles, hula-hoops, and blue jeans. While cars, toys, and clothing were not new, the way in which most teenagers first heard about them was. Instead of reading about them in catalogs, newspapers, and magazines as their parents had before them, young people in the 1950s first heard about them on television.

An advertisement for Motorola TV. (Library of Congress)

Companies advertising these new products saw baby boomers as the ideal audience. Advertisers also found that television, which had not existed in most homes until the early 1950s, was the ideal way to reach them. By the mid-1950s, nine out of ten American households owned a TV. Soon the programs and advertising on TV began to shape the nation's attitudes, what it bought, what it wore, and how it thought about world and national issues. Although some people still struggled, most Americans had money left over after the basic necessities were paid for. This extra money, or disposable income, helped people buy many of the things they wanted, including new cars, cigarettes, soft drinks, chewing gum, sugar-coated cereals with toys in the box—and new televisions.

Despite fears about the atomic bomb, the Cold War, and racial unrest, the 1950s were a time of opportunity for many. The trend continued toward building communities of single-family homes within commuting distance of America's cities. In the 1950s, what had become known as suburbia grew faster than any other residential area. By 1959, almost one-third of the population—mostly white—lived in suburbs. These communities included shopping centers, schools, factories, offices, houses of worship, and fast-food restaurants. Hurriedly built roads created a wide pattern of development, often without traditional town centers. Since one community often merged seamlessly into the next, this was called suburban sprawl.

To live in the suburbs, one needed to own a car, and during the 1950s, Americans were more mobile than ever. A growing network of interstate highways, called superhighways, began to link the nation, further stimulating automobile purchases and travel. In 1940, there had been 32 million motor vehicles in the United States, 27 million of them passenger cars. By 1959, there were 74 million motor vehicles, 62 million of them passenger cars.

With the growing use of cars, the number of people using public transportation such as buses, subways, and rail commuter lines declined drastically, even in cities. Cars created traffic jams during the morning and evening "rush hours" when people were coming and going to and from work.

The Eisenhower Presidency

Born in Texas and brought up in Kansas, Republican Dwight D. Eisenhower had been supreme commander of Allied troops in World War II. In his 1952 campaign for president, Eisenhower offered to go to Korea, where peace talks had stalled.

Eisenhower brought optimism and a conservative middle-of-the-road approach to governing. He won a large number of votes from once-staunch Democrats, including many from labor unions and black city dwellers. He defeated his Democratic opponent, Adlai Stevenson, by 33.8 million to 27.3 million votes in 1952. In 1956, he again beat Stevenson by a more decisive 35.5 million to 25.7 million.

A campaign button for Dwight D. Eisenhower that uses his nickname, "Ike." (private collection)

After being elected but before taking office, Eisenhower went to Korea as promised. He threatened to extend the war into China and to use small-scale atomic weapons, but the talks remained stalled. Seven months later, however, the two sides agreed to quit fighting.

Eisenhower suffered a heart attack in 1955, which weakened him. Still, he had the strong will to order American troops to Lebanon in 1958 to oppose communist rebels. He sent National Guard troops to Arkansas to prevent violence during racial integration of public schools.

In his diplomatic efforts to better relations with other nations, Eisenhower invited Russian leader Nikita Khrushchev to visit America. It was the first-ever Cold War "summit meeting" between the leaders of the world's top powers. Khrushchev was far less threatening than Stalin, who had died in 1953. Periodically, "summits" were held to maintain peace and to address critical disputes and rivalries.

There were many areas of fierce competition between the Soviet Union and the United States—from Olympic sports to the race to explore outer space. During the Cold War, each accomplishment was used by each side to prove that its system of government was superior.

The effort to be the first to launch an artificial satellite into orbit around the earth pitted each country's best scientists and industries against the other. The USSR succeeded first in October 1957, sending up *Sputnik I*. This achievement created a panic among some Americans. They feared that if Russians could launch a satellite the size of a basketball, they could send an atomic bomb with the same missile. In November, the USSR sent up *Sputnik II*. They put a dog named Laika on board, although they had no way to recover him, and he died. Eisenhower counseled patience. In January 1958, the United States launched its own satellite, and the space race was on. The ultimate goal was to send up and bring back a manned space vehicle safely.

One particular American technological success in this era was much less prominent than the space program: the development of computers. The first electronic calculator had been built in 1946. Scientists were amazed to see an early digital computer working out, in two hours, nuclear physics calculations that would have required a hundred engineers a full year to do. Computers were becoming ever more powerful and faster, bearing promise of a mighty technical revolution to come.

New Borders, New Generation

In the two decades from 1941 to 1960, the U.S. population increased from 132 million to 179 million. There was much good feeling in 1959, when Alaska and Hawaii entered the Union as the forty-ninth and fiftieth states. The United States now had brought the last western frontiers within its national borders.

By now, teenage baby boomers had their own ideas. Having grown up with many material comforts, they sought other things. Idealists in this younger generation hoped to see an end to the Cold War. They believed the United States had the power to make the world a far better place in which to live. Young people began to question American foreign policies that supported dictatorships. Also, some young whites began to ally themselves with blacks, resolving to work together for integration and understanding between the races.

By 1960, baby boomers were perhaps the best-educated, best-cared-for, and most prosperous American generation of all. The world they would inherit, the world they were about to help shape, continued to change swiftly, and many embraced that change.

In the 1960 presidential elections, 43-year-old Massachusetts senator John F. Kennedy defeated two-term Vice President Richard M. Nixon, who was 47. This presidential campaign was the first in which television was key to the outcome.

The candidates debated in live broadcasts viewed by most of the nation. Kennedy's good looks, humor, and willingness to wear makeup to appear tan are considered to have given him an edge over Nixon. Nixon refused makeup and appeared nervous on camera. The election was remarkably close, with Kennedy winning by the slimmest of margins: 118,550 popular votes in a total of 86.3 million cast. The final tally was 43.2 million to 43.1 million.

Vice President Richard M. Nixon, in Los Angeles, debates Senator John F. Kennedy, in New York, in the first live televised presidential debate in 1960. Surveys showed that most of those who heard the debate on radio felt Nixon had won. Those who watched on television thought Kennedy had won. (Library of Congress)

Chapter One

Family Life

Americans at home anxiously followed news reports about the war raging overseas. With more than 16 million men and women in the military service, almost every family lived with the fear that loved ones would never return or would be seriously wounded. That worry cast a cloud over the country, but life had to go on.

New workers took the places of those who were away in the war, and new jobs paying high wages opened up in the war industry. Yet even if people had the cash to spend, there was a shortage of food, consumer goods, and housing. Most of the nation's industrial and agricultural production was directed to the war effort, for equipment and to supply the troops. For this reason, civilians often found store shelves almost bare.

To keep prices from rising too fast and creating inflation, the government placed controls on what could be charged for many things that were available. Household appliances, used cars, and even bicycles had price controls.

By 1943, during the middle of the war, Americans faced shortages of everything from gasoline to sewing machines, sugar to hair curlers. Many goods were not produced during this time because they were considered "nonessential" to the military effort or were needed for the war. Women could not buy silk stockings, for example, because silk was used to make para-

After Japan attacked Pearl Harbor in 1941, the United States ordered more than 100,000 Japanese Americans living on the West Coast to leave their homes to live in guarded "internment camps." The government did this to prevent Japanese Americans from spying for Japan. Many of those interned, like the Hirano family (LEFT), had sons serving in the U.S. military. (National Archives) While many women worked during the war in defense plants, after the war, many married returning soldiers, settled in new suburbs, and became housewives (RIGHT). (Hulton Archives)

chutes. This was a major problem in a day when most women wore skirts and dresses, and bare legs were considered unattractive. Some women used makeup on their legs, even drawing a line down the calf to simulate stocking seams.

Military production required metals that were normally used in automobiles, household utensils, construction, and even in beer cans and bottle caps. The manufacture of these items almost stopped during the war, or else they were in short supply. When replacements for older machines and utensils could not be found, people made do with what they had. They repaired worn-out objects they might once have thrown away.

Nationwide "scrap drives" were held to help supply the military need for steel, iron, tin, and copper. These drives collected old equipment, tools, fences, roofs, and even iron statues for recycling into usable metals. Families cleaned out garages, basements, backyards, and barns to contribute when the scrap-metal trucks came by. A good scrap drive proved that a community could support the war effort.

Families learned not to waste anything, especially food. The military needed at least one-fourth of the food the nation produced. What was left was sold to the public. Coffee and sugar were expensive, because they came from other countries, normally by sea. This was a dangerous business, because enemy submarines sank thousands of merchant ships during the war. Coffee grounds were reused several times before they were thrown away. A coffee substitute was made from a combination of chicory and grains. Corn syrup was used instead of sugar. Cigarettes, a habit of most adults, went by the millions to the military, making it hard for civilians to find them.

To make sure civilians shared fairly in whatever was available for purchase, the government created a system of rationing. Rationing limited how much a person could buy. Each month, every American adult and child received ration books with stamps that were to be torn off and given to the seller whenever certain items were purchased. Each stamp allowed the buyer a certain amount of groceries, meats, dairy, and also automobile products and gasoline. If stamps were used up, a buyer had to wait until next month's ration book arrived to make new purchases.

Stamps were often traded like cash. For example, if a family

Car-sharing clubs were formed during World War II to help conserve fuel. (Library of Congress)

raised chickens and did not need meat-ration stamps, it could trade those stamps to someone who had extra gasoline stamps and wanted meat stamps.

To make sure they had enough fresh vegetables, Americans planted their own garden plots. These were called "Victory Gardens" because they helped the national war effort by feeding civilians. Victory Gardens were found everywhere, on the edge of small towns and in the middle of cities. Some were in parks or vacant lots, and others were planted on front lawns, on rooftops, and even along the busy sidewalks of Manhattan.

Many newcomers to the city had moved there from the countryside, so they had plenty of experience in vegetable growing. Finding a home in wartime, however, was more difficult than getting enough food.

New Lives, New Hope, No Place to Live

By early in the war, more than 2 million Americans had moved to cities like Los Angeles and San Francisco, California and Mobile, Alabama, where military manufacturing boomed and jobs were waiting.

Many of the 15.3 million Americans who migrated during the war went to fast-growing metropolitan areas in California, Washington State, and Oregon. A large number went to industrialized cities in Michigan and Illinois. These people did not only come from rural areas. Hundreds of thousands left the older cities of the East and went to the West and South. The New York City region lost 800,000 residents, Pittsburgh 200,000, and Boston 150,000.

In new industrial areas, decent places to live were quickly taken. Housing prices and rents rose fast when a flood of newcomers arrived. Both apartments and single-family homes were in short supply. Young couples, perhaps with a child or two, often shared living quarters with other families to help to pay the rent. Young families who stayed in their own towns sometimes moved in with parents. They might sleep on a daybed in the living room

Many Americans planted "Victory Gardens" for extra food, since much of the food grown on farms was sent to feed U.S. soldiers overseas.
(Library of Congress)

or convert a porch into a bedroom. Others crowded into tiny apartments, shared space in run-down trailer camps, or lived in converted barns, garages, storefronts, and even chicken coops.

Many young couples married during the war. Marriage rates were the highest in American history, at approximately 12.2 marriages per thousand population. This represented about 1.6 million weddings a year. Tens of thousands of families followed their servicemen husbands and fathers as they were transferred from base to base in the United States. The military gave them only $50 a month, hardly enough to live on. Servicemen's families lived wherever they could find housing in the towns and villages around the bases. The men had to get permission to visit their families for a couple of days each month. When servicemen shipped out overseas, the families stayed behind, never knowing how long they would be separated.

For African American civilians who moved by the thousands from the rural South to the cities of the North, housing was especially hard to find. Racial segregation meant that black Americans could only find homes in certain districts of a city or town. These quickly became overcrowded as new families moved in. Although the federal government built many "housing projects," as new apartment buildings were called, most were for whites only. The number of housing projects for blacks did not meet the needs of major cities, such as Detroit, where 60,000 African Americans arrived during the war years.

A great many black families improved their incomes thanks to jobs in the war industry, but they still had to live in substandard housing. Most were forced to live in black-only neighborhoods where many people lived in poverty. No matter what their race, most migrants found themselves in new, unfamiliar surroundings. They were often lonely, without the support of family and friends who remained at home or had gone somewhere else to seek opportunity. The lure of higher pay and a better life was a powerful attraction, though. Americans tried to make the best of a difficult situation. They struggled on day after day in the hope that it all soon would be worth it.

Women Earn Good Pay as Prices Rise

Many people found well-paying jobs when they moved to the cities where war manufacturing was booming. Since employers could not get enough workers, women and teenagers went into the job market full-time, as never before. Women took jobs that until then had been considered men's work. They became skilled equipment operators, worked in manufacturing and on the assembly line, managed offices, and helped build warships, tanks, and planes.

American families had more cash on hand. It was expected that daily life would be better as a result, but inflation pushed the cost of living steadily up. Higher earnings did not always meet the higher costs caused by shortages of goods and housing and by inflation.

One additional cost for many working mothers was the price of temporary day care for their children. There was little organized day care during World War II, and what there was could be expensive. To avoid this cost, families often left children with grandparents or neighbors.

After the Allied victory in 1945, those in the military service were discharged at the rate of a million a month. Many wartime marriages failed when the husband returned after being away for years. In 1945, more than 485,000 marriages ended in divorce, a rate of 3.5 per thousand population. This compared to 264,000 divorces in 1940, for a rate of 2.0 per thousand. But the majority of American couples were happy to be reunited. They soon discov-

Women at the Long Beach, California, plant of Douglas Aircraft Company clean off the noses of new A-20 bomber planes. (National Archives)

ered that finding housing would be even more difficult. The "baby boom" of the mid-1940s further increased the demand for homes.

The Rise of Suburbia

A year or two after the war, things began to change for the better in housing. The federal government's loan programs for military veterans started the greatest housing growth ever seen in the United States. Government loans made it possible for families to buy the single-family homes of their dreams.

By now, many young parents had been able to save money to help buy their own homes. This was partly thanks to forced saving during the war, when there was so little to buy. Also, many had bought war bonds, a government program to raise money for the military effort. Money invested in war bonds was paid back after the war and was added to the family's savings. These savings, combined with new government loans, made the World War II generation ready and able to buy homes.

In the late 1940s, builders had a way to supply those homes by building them quickly in "housing developments" outside the cities. In 1949, construction companies on Long Island, New York, began to create thousands of look-alike houses that were affordable for young families. Homes in a development were almost identical in style, with the same basic floor plans. These houses often did not have basements, which saved in the cost of construction. To save money, all the houses in some developments were painted in the same color.

These communities of inexpensive, one-family homes shaped America's fast-growing suburbs during the 1940s and 1950s. Suburban development homes were small, but they were more comfortable than shared homes or housing project apartments. Developments offered private backyards and barbecue pits, with streets that were quiet and crime-free. They were ideal neighborhoods for middle-class families, who began moving out of cities into these "bedroom communities," as they were called. Suburban towns earned this name because parents usually went to the city to work and came home to sleep.

The rapid growth of "suburbia" was one of the most important social changes in the years after World War II and through the 1950s. As millions of Americans left the cities for the suburbs, so did many businesses, industry, and retailers. Business followed

Levittown: A Modest Dream House

Young American parents who came of age during World War II had known mostly hard times since their childhoods in the Great Depression of the 1930s. Now they had dreams of a better life.They were eager to have their own homes with a plot of land where three or four children could happily play. Their dream home would be in the country, a Cape Cod–style or a ranch house, modest and small. There would be a detached garage for the family car.

Between 1946 and 1955, the pioneering construction company Levitt and Sons, Inc., fulfilled that dream for thousands of families from New York to Pennsylvania. The first development established by company president William J. Levitt was on farmland in Nassau County, Long Island. Known as Levittown, it opened for business in March 1949, offering buyers a 25 x 30-square-foot house with four rooms and a yard for less than $7,000. Since the federal government was financing the mortgages as part of a nationwide housing program, no down payment was needed from ex-servicemen and their wives. They eagerly lined up to make their purchases.

To meet the huge demand, these homes had to be built quickly and inexpensively. Parts were manufactured in factories: interior walls, trusses, windows, and doors arrived on the building site ready for quick installation. These were followed, according to a tightly organized schedule, by deliveries of sheetrock, paint, bathroom and kitchen fixtures, and lighting. Built in a matter of days, these homes solved the desperate national shortage of housing. At the same time,

they gave this generation a start that no other Americans had ever received.

Imitators of mass-produced Levittown developments sprang up all around the country. Between 1948 and 1958, more than 13 million homes were built in the United States, 11 million of them in the suburbs. By 1970, the eastern Pennsylvania community incorporated under the name Levittown had 80,000 residents, and the original Nassau County development had grown to more than 65,000.

Levittown, on Long Island, New York, was founded in the late 1940s. While the row after row of inexpensive and almost identical houses may not have been as attractive as the neighborhoods in older communities, they made owning a home affordable. (Library of Congress)

A freeway interchange outside of Los Angeles, California, in the 1950s. (Hulton-Getty Archive)

the well-to-do middle-class population. Shopping malls were rapidly built in "strips" along new roads and highways that joined the housing developments to the cities. Each year, roads were extended farther outward, like the threads of a web. New countryside became the next ring of suburbs.

Cars were essential to getting around in the suburbs. The automobile became a way of life, and it seemed everyone was in the car and on the run. Drive-in movies were popular, and drive-in restaurants appeared in many strip malls. The food served at drive-ins was cooked and served quickly, earning it the name "fast food." As families grew larger, the standard one-car garage was not enough. Then they moved farther out to larger homes with more garage space and bigger lawns.

Suburban families had all the modern conveniences, such as the latest telephones and appliances. In the early 1950s, television replaced radio as the center of the home, although many of radio's comedies, dramas, and musical and variety shows moved over to television. Familiar radio performers such as comedians Jack Benny and Milton Berle became television hits, and filmmakers found a fast-growing audience among television viewers.

Television was so much the center of daily home life that a new way of eating appeared. The "TV dinner" was a package of precooked frozen food, ready for heating up. Instead of gathering around a table together, family members could quickly cook TV dinners and sit down in front of the television set. This way, they never missed their favorite shows.

Life beyond Suburbia

By the mid-1950s, America had changed drastically because of the rise of suburbia. The cities were decaying while the suburbs blossomed.

City life lost much of its strength and energy. When a large portion of the middle class moved to the suburbs, the cities became poorer. City governments found it difficult to raise money from taxes. While modern schools and municipal buildings were going up in the suburbs, cities were forced to cut back on education and public services such as transportation. Neighborhoods suffered because the cities did not have enough funds for police, fire, and sanitation.

A middle-class family in a Los Angeles or New Jersey suburban neighborhood could enjoy a comfortable life if the father had a good job in a defense plant. These plants had plenty of business now that the country was spending millions to fight the Cold War (see Chapter 2). For many other people, however, things were not so promising.

A farm in Haskell County, Kansas, in 1941. (National Archives)

On the family farms of the Midwest, daily life demanded extremely hard work, seven days a week. In this time, farm-product prices steadily declined because the family farm had stiff competition from huge agricultural operations. As the future of the independent farm dimmed, young family members moved to the city to work for a steady salary. Farmers watched their children leave, knowing there would be no one to take over the homestead when they retired.

In Baltimore, an African American family that had moved up from a South Carolina farm might find plenty of employment, but it would be forced to live in a racially segregated neighbor-

During World War II, these women found work on the Baltimore & Ohio Railroad. (National Archives)

hood. Here, young residents often felt deep hostility and resentment because they had little educational opportunity and hardly any chance to move to a better neighborhood. These communities were called ghettos, meaning a place where a certain group of people is forced to live separately from the rest of the population. Since few saw any way out, the abuse of alcohol and drugs rose in these neighborhoods, as did crime.

Native Americans on the nation's many reservations had even fewer economic opportunities than blacks. Living in poorly built government housing, far from major cities, Indians had no way to earn a good living. They had little chance to improve their situation unless they moved off the reservation. Many thousands did just that, but they often faced harsh bigotry. To find work and be accepted by whites, they sometimes concealed their native roots and raised their children with little knowledge of their people's heritage.

Hispanics, mainly Mexican Americans and Puerto Ricans, kept up their cultures and their languages as they worked to share in the country's growing prosperity. They also faced prejudice and racism, and their families struggled through it with determination and hard work. Many Mexican Americans took low-wage agriculture jobs. As migrant farmworkers, they traveled around harvesting fruit and field crops. They often sent part of their earnings to Mexico, where they had family members. Puerto Ricans established dynamic communities in New York City's formerly Italian or Irish neighborhoods, abandoned in the rush to the suburbs.

In the hamlets and small cabins of the Appalachian Mountains, most jobs were to be found in the dark, dangerous caverns of coal mines. In Appalachia, as elsewhere, young people looking for opportunity had to leave home and go to the cities. They usually headed north to Illinois and Ohio, settling with other migrants from their home counties who had moved up before them. Appalachian people preserved their culture, and country and bluegrass music developed from their folkways. Some of this music merged with black rhythm and blues to create a new sound that was called "rock 'n' roll."

In this time, one part of the population was happy to be in the American cities. These were several million European refugees. Uprooted by the war, they emigrated to the United States and moved into neighborhoods where their ethnic group or nationality already lived. They, too, tried to keep up their customs and traditions. In places like Chicago and Newark, New Jersey, recent European immigrants found acceptance among their own folk, who had established themselves twenty or thirty years earlier. In big cities, neighborhoods of Poles or Ukrainians or Croats or German Jews preserved much of their heritage and language. Their children grew up as Americans who knew both cultures.

Inventions, Time-savers, and Over-stressed Parents

The war effort produced dozens of new materials that were first used by the military and then adapted to America's daily needs. The Rubbermaid company, for example, produced life jackets for the navy and leak-proof gas tanks for fighter planes. Rubbermaid's technology developed a new form of plastic containers and utensils that were ideal for household purposes. A wartime inventor developed a clear polymer plastic to wrap machine guns for shipment, keeping them from rusting. He named this wrap after his two daughters, Sarah and Ann. In the 1940s, Saran Wrap was found to be perfect for keeping food fresh. Another industrial material used for household purposes was the glassware known as Pyrex. This material was first used in signal lanterns before its name became famous for cookware resistant to heat and cold.

By the early 1950s, inventions and kitchen gadgets made daily

Marriage, Divorce, and Family Size

After World War II, as couples reunited at the return of the servicemen, many realized they had married too impulsively, and there was a sudden rise in divorces.

Although divorce was scandalous at the time, more than 485,000 couples went through with it in 1945, compared with 264,000 divorces in 1940.

The divorce rate in 1945 was 3.5 divorces per thousand population, and only 2.0 per thousand in 1940. The number of divorces would drop by 25 percent by 1950 and stay at that level for the next decade before rising again.

From 1945 to 1960, the total number of marriages hovered between 1.45 million to 1.6 million each year. In this same period, family size ranged between 3.5 to 3.6 persons each.

The birthrate rose from 19.4 births per thousand population in 1940 to a high of 26.6 in 1947. It had dropped to 23.7 by 1960.

life easier for the American housewife. Aluminum foil appeared in this era, as did the toaster oven, the pet door, and the movable barbecue grill. Still, the woman of the house never had enough time to do all the work at hand. Though she had the latest washer and dryer, dishwasher, refrigerator, mixers, telephones, and a car of her own, the suburban mother was caught up in a whirlwind of activity and work. Research showed she was putting more time into housework, child care, and shopping than did mothers of previous generations.

Society demanded the most from the modern mother. She was expected to do everything well, from homemaking to raising children. The father was expected to be a good provider, be there when needed, fix things in the household, play sports with the son, and be a wise mentor to the children. In the suburbs, however, he generally was at work all day. The harried mother drove the children back and forth to events and lessons. She volunteered at school for the PTA and for charities. She played the expert hostess and cook for dinners with friends and neighbors. Through it all, the woman was required to be an excellent mate to her husband, helping to advance his career. She was not expected to think about any career for herself outside the home.

Many women had tasted the independence of working and earning their own money during World War II. At the end of the war, they had given up their jobs to the returning servicemen and become obedient wives and devoted mothers. In suburbia, especially, women were far from the liveliness of the city. Many found themselves lonely because their husbands were away so much. Too often, women were unable to find fulfillment in the life they and their husbands had tried to make in their dream home.

According to the latest theories of child care, the mother was the one most responsible for her family's emotional and physical health. Advice books written by specialists such as pediatrician Dr. Benjamin Spock said the mother was the key to a happy home. This meant that if children had problems, then it was probably the fault of the mother. She somehow had failed. This enormous pressure on women in the 1950s was condemned by feminists. They said the mother was being unfairly blamed for everything that went wrong in the family.

Television presented the happy American family, but the average housewife could not keep up with the ideal woman she was expected to copy. Her children could try to be smart and funny like Beaver Cleaver in *Leave it to Beaver*. And for the few hours a day that her husband was at home, he could try to be as sensible as Jim Anderson in *Father Knows Best* or Ozzie Nelson in *The Adventures of Ozzie and Harriet.* It was the mother and wife, however, who had the heaviest day-to-day burden of raising the family.

Pressures on the father came from another direction. Many men were frustrated after years of commuting to jobs that were unsatisfying. Others threw themselves into their careers so completely that there was no time for their families. Husbands were also troubled as they became aware of the unhappiness of their wives, who wanted more from life.

Further, fathers were portrayed on television as bumbling fellows who were not he strong role models they once had been. Situation comedies such as *The Life of Riley* and *Blondie* portrayed Americans father figures who were incompetent, though well-meaning and lovable. On television, the father did not know best anymore, and his children often treated him rudely. The real-life father was losing his place as the honored head of the American family.

Children, on the other hand, often were portrayed on television and in popular psychology books as being brighter than their parents and with far more common sense. Traditional roles and family relationships were changing fast by the close of the 1950s. At the same time, the young people, called "baby boomers," were growing up more confident and independent-minded than any generation in history.

Television's Cleaver family, starring Jerry Mathers as the youngest son, Beaver, presented one view of the ideal television family. (Library of Congress)

We Can Do It!

Chapter Two

Social and Political Attitudes

During World War II, millions of women went to work in American factories to help produce supplies needed for the war effort. The poster above (LEFT) celebrates the effort of America's women. In 1952, General Dwight D. Eisenhower (RIGHT), who had commanded the Allied forces in Europe during the war, was elected president. His reassuring personality made him a popular president. (Library of Congress)

In 1940, American public opinion and most politicians were strongly against going to war. Yet the country did much to help Britain fight against Nazi Germany during that first full year of what was becoming World War II.

President Franklin D. Roosevelt often said that he opposed Americans being sent to foreign wars. At the same time, he expressed concern that if the fascists won in Europe, the United States would be threatened next.

A large part of the population demanded that the United States never again be drawn into foreign wars. People who took this stand were termed isolationists. They wanted to keep the country free of political entanglements with other nations. In 1940, isolationists numbered about one-third of the population. One of the best-organized isolationist groups was the America First Committee. Its members were known as "America Firsters." Their stand was to account for the security of the United States first, no matter what happened to other countries.

When President Roosevelt called for a military draft in 1940, the America Firsters bitterly opposed it. Congress saw the need to strengthen the national defense. It adopted the first peacetime draft in American history. Isolationists were even more furious when Roosevelt began a massive military buildup. European Allies, such as Belgium and France, were defeated, and Britain was under siege. Many Americans realized the Atlantic Ocean might not be enough to protect them.

American military development grew even faster after Roosevelt was reelected to a third term in 1940. Roosevelt won 54 percent of the popular vote, 27.2 million to Republican Wendell L. Willkie's 22.3 million. Public opinion now favored a strong American military and also supported Roosevelt's program of supplying Britain. By mid-1941, Congress had financed this military policy with more than $6.6 billion.

The president now had the power to prepare for war and assist Britain. Because of America's great military manufacturing output, the country became known as the "arsenal of democracy."

Racism and Anti-Semitism

The nation was taken by surprise in December 1941, when Japan attacked the naval base at Pearl Harbor, Hawaii. Now public opinion was almost unanimously in favor of all-out war.

As the country went to war against Japan and the European fascists, deep hostility developed against Japanese Americans. There was anger against German and Italian Americans as well, but feelings were most harsh against Japanese Americans. More than 120,000 Americans of Japanese ancestry were put into internment camps, even though most had lived here all their lives and were citizens. They lost their homes, businesses, and jobs and were accused of being enemy aliens. The government believed many might secretly aid Japan's military by spying or committing acts of sabotage.

German Americans and Italian Americans were not singled out for such treatment. This showed the deep prejudice of mainstream America against Asians, or Orientals, as they were called. Although there had been deep prejudice against Germans during World War I, European Americans were now trusted to be loyal. Resentment against Asians had been widespread in America since the mid-1800s. White prejudice against the Chinese and Japanese came in large part because those populations worked hard and grew rapidly, becoming prosperous. Strict federal immigration quotas had been placed on Asians in the 1920s.

As World War II progressed, the early fears of Japanese Americans passed. The nation settled into a state of war. People were gradually allowed to leave the internment camps. Many were determined to prove that they were loyal to the country. Thousands enlisted in the military and proved to be among the finest troops in American history. One army unit made up of Hawaiians and Japanese Americans won more medals than any other in the U.S. armed services.

Despite the contribution of racial minorities during the war, the country maintained strict immigration policies that favored Europeans over all others. The one exception to this policy were European Jews. Prejudice against Jews, called anti-Semitism, was strong during this era. In 1938, a public opinion poll showed that 53 percent of those polled favored restricting the rights of Jews in American society. Jobs were advertised for "Christians Only," and Jewish doctors were not allowed to practice in mainstream hospitals. Many clubs, beaches, and schools discriminated against Jews.

This prejudice had terrible consequences for Jews trying to flee Nazi persecution. In 1939, Congress failed to pass the Wagner-Rogers bill that would have rescued Jewish children from war-torn Europe. That same year, the United States refused to intervene on the part of a

Before the war, some German Americans, like the members of the German American Bund seen marching in New York City (RIGHT), actively supported the Nazi government of Adolf Hitler. The U.S. government used Dorothy Waring ("Secret Agent 89") and others to spy on German American groups during the war. The poster above advertises one of her speeches. (Library of Congress

ship full of Jews who had fled to Cuba. The Cuban government refused to let them land, and they were forced to return to Europe. As Hitler moved toward his "final solution" to eliminate all European Jews, Nazism claimed 25,000 U.S. supporters who held parades and rallies across the nation. Father Charles Coughlin made weekly radio broadcasts blaming the Jews for all of America's problems. It would later be revealed that the U.S. State Department had actively worked to prevent Jews from immigrating to the United States and had withheld information about the Nazi persecution.

African Americans were also treated as second-class citizens. Even the military was segregated by race, with blacks serving in their own units. Like the Japanese Americans, though, black servicemen proved the equal of whites. An all-black fighter squadron became the most decorated in the air force.

By the end of the war, American racial minorities had achieved much in the way of economic improvement. They had better paying jobs during the war and also proved themselves by defending the country. Blacks, in particular, wanted the full civil rights they had fought and worked to defend during World War II.

Women, too, were changed by the war. Not only did thousands join the service, but millions went to work. Women saw their lives could change. They saw that they could do jobs that until then had been considered "men's work." After World War II, the stage was set for women and minorities to demand more rights and more freedoms.

The Changing Face of Politics

Roosevelt's Democrats were solidly in power in the early 1940s. They had especially strong support from labor, urban blacks, and the South. Although many Americans believed Roosevelt had too much power, the general population supported him. He was reelected for a fourth term in 1944. He won with 25.6 million popular votes to 22 million for New York governor Thomas E. Dewey, the Republican candidate.

Vice President Harry S Truman became president when Roosevelt suddenly died in the spring of 1945. Although he came from the border state of Missouri, Truman promoted civil rights for blacks. In 1948, he officially ended racial segregation in the U.S. military. His policies for integration earned him hostility in the South. It also split the Democratic Party. A faction of southerners broke off to call themselves "Dixiecrats."

Dixiecrats demanded more power for the states and less for the federal government. They opposed antisegregation laws and declared that federal authorities were creating a police state by enforcing those laws. In the 1948 presidential election, the Dixiecrats ran their own candidate, South Carolina governor Strom Thurmond. Thurmond took many votes from the Democrats and Truman, who again faced Republican Dewey of New York.

Another national party entered the 1948 presidential race: the Progressive Party. Calling for an easing of tensions between the United States and the Soviet Union, the Progressives nominated former Roosevelt vice president Henry A. Wallace. The press predicted Truman would lose the election, but he won with a popular vote of 24.1 million to Dewey's 21.9 million. Thurmond and Wallace received about 1.6 million votes each.

Although Truman won the 1948 election, the Democratic Party was permanently split. In years to come, many Dixiecrats would join the Republican Party.

Racial Attitudes Change Slowly

After World War II, Americans were shocked to learn of the Nazi genocide that had murdered millions in Europe, including 6 million Jews.

In January 1943, President Roosevelt had set up the War Refugee Board, which helped rescue as many as 200,000 Jews. The nation learned the terrible lesson that racial or religious prejudice could lead to unthinkable evil.

Despite these lessons, the United States continued to have its own racial tensions. Jim Crow laws forbade interracial marriage. They required segregation in public places: schools, trains, buses, restaurants, hotels, and theaters. Sports, too, were segregated, although college football teams often had black players. Professional football had a number of star African American players by 1946. But baseball leagues were firmly all-white or all-black. This division between races was called a "color line."

The nation admired black heavyweight boxing champion Joe Louis, who rose to fame in the 1940s. Yet team sports remained segregated because many whites did not want to associate with blacks. They did not want to travel or dine with blacks, and hotels often refused black customers. Although the North did not have segregation laws, many baseball fans in those states opposed blacks on professional teams. Eventually, black athletic talent won the day. Many outstanding baseball players were playing in the professional Negro Leagues. White club owners and coaches wanted these skilled players on their own teams. But most feared racial prejudice would cause too much trouble with the fans.

Then, in 1947, Branch Rickey, owner of the Brooklyn Dodgers, took a courageous step. Rickey signed outfielder Jackie Robinson, who stood up to insults and abuse and became rookie of the year. One by one, great black stars joined formerly all-white baseball teams, leading the way to integration in sports and society. Pitcher Leroy "Satchel" Paige also joined the major leagues. Black stars such as Robinson and Paige helped their clubs win, and the fans, black and white, soon enthusiastically supported them.

Meanwhile, the winning of civil rights for African Americans was a slow and painful process. One of the most notable successes came in 1949, when the University of Arkansas Medical

During the Civil Rights movement that started in the 1950s, demonstrators used "nonviolent resistance" to win civil rights. In 1960, black students in Greensboro, North Carolina sat at a "whites only" Woolworths lunch counter and refused to leave. Rather than serve them, the lunch counter closed. (Library of Congress)

School accepted its first black student: Edith Mae Irby. This was the beginning of a long-term effort to integrate Southern colleges.

In these years, racial hostility and unrest accompanied the movement toward integration in the South. Young blacks sat down at white-only lunch counters and were promptly arrested. Others held peaceful demonstrations outside white-only establishments. They were often attacked by police and civilians. Despite the risks, the Civil Rights movement gathered strength across the country. One great victory was won in 1954, when the U.S. Supreme Court ruled against segregation in public schools.

In 1957, President Eisenhower had to send troops to Little Rock, Arkansas, to keep the peace when nine black students tried to attend the all-white high school. Integration of schools would take place only slowly. It required ten more years for complete school desegregation in Little Rock.

The Civil Rights movement's single most prominent incident took place on a bus in Montgomery, Alabama, in 1955. Rosa Parks refused to give up her seat to a white person and move to the back of the bus. Her arrest sparked a boycott of buses by anti-segregationists led by a young Baptist minister, Martin Luther King, Jr. The boycott was dedicated to nonviolent resistance, even though many protesters were threatened by racists and police.

The standoff was finally resolved by the U.S. Supreme Court. A year after the bus boycott began, the court declared racial segregation of public transportation to be illegal. This decision resulted in desegregation of the bus lines. Now African Americans could sit where they wanted on public buses, trolleys, or trains.

The Red Scare

In the late 1940s and first years of the 1950s, Americans were worried about the possibility of communist spies secretly operating in the United States. In the previous ten years, the nation had left isolationism behind, and now it was one of the two most powerful countries on earth. Victory in World War II had created a new world, divided into East and West, or communist and noncommunist.

The United States confronted the communist Soviet Union, which controlled Eastern Europe. Also, a communist government had taken over China. Americans feared communist takeovers elsewhere. It seemed the threat was on all sides of the globe. Further, the Soviet Union had acquired atomic weapons and was capable of destroying the United States in an atomic war.

Many Americans came to believe that communists were everywhere, trying to bring down democracy. Scientists, diplomats, professors, writers, filmmakers, and ordinary workers were suspected and accused of being communists. Many people who had been idealistic young socialists in the 1930s were falsely accused of being subversive enemy agents.

Congressional hearings were held to investigate the "communist threat," and witnesses were required to testify or else be imprisoned. In 1947, the House Un-American Activities Committee investigated many individuals. Some admitted they believed in the goals of communism or socialism, but declared they did not want to undermine the American government. Others made sometimes false accusations against colleagues and friends in order to prove themselves anticommunist. Still others refused to testify by invoking the Constitution's Fifth Amendment protection against self-incrimination.

One group that stood up against the congressional hearings were called the "Hollywood Ten." These film producers, directors, and screenwriters opposed the government's scare tactics. They were prosecuted, and some were jailed when they refused to answer to whether or not they were communists. Many in Hollywood and the arts and also journalists were put on a government "black list" to prevent them ever again working in the media.

Many careers were destroyed unjustly. What became known

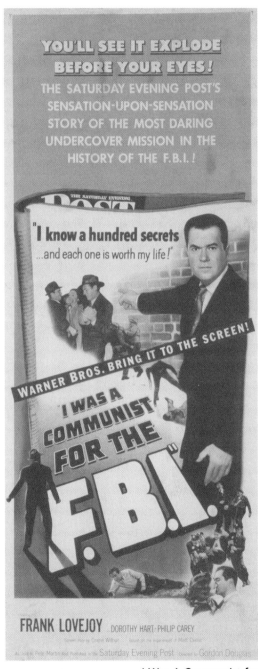

I Was A Communist for the FBI, a film released at the height of the "Red Scare" of the early 1950s.
(Library of Congress)

Senator Joseph R. McCarthy, who lead the Senate's investigations into communism in the United States, receives a gift of "Northern Spie" apples from a Canadian apple grower. (Library of Congress)

as the "Red Scare" gave average Americans a real sense of fear that communism was everywhere. Secret agents, Americans believed, were even in the government and military. Republican senator Joseph McCarthy of Wisconsin took advantage of this paranoia. McCarthy led a campaign of false accusations and slander against those he said were secret communists. Many were smeared with the accusation of being communists. He even accused President Truman and much-decorated George C. Marshall, the chief of the general staff, of leaning toward communism.

From 1950 to 1954, McCarthy riveted the attention of the American public. Though he had no proof and sometimes created false evidence, McCarthy had the public platform of a Senate subcommittee. He took advantage of the American fear of communism to build up his own political power. Many politicians dreaded that he would attack them next. His campaign of lies and slander helped to defeat several Democratic senators in their reelection bids.

"McCarthyism," as his view of the world was called, became so powerful that the federal government prepared six new detention camps to imprison spies and subversives. At the same time, McCarthy won support among many Republicans, whose party had not held the presidency for twenty years. With the Korean War taking thousands of American lives in the early 1950s, Americans were even more set against communism.

Joseph McCarthy made a fatal error in 1954 when he threatened to investigate the army. President Eisenhower instructed the army to expose McCarthy's threats in hearings held by his subcommittee. Televised across the nation, the Army-McCarthy hearings were electrifying. In the end, McCarthy exposed himself as a bullying liar when he attacked one of the young lawyers on the army's staff.

The climax came when the army's special counsel, Joseph Welch, could no longer stand the vicious attack on his young colleague. Welch said, "Little did I dream you could be so reckless or so cruel as to do injury to that lad . . . . Have you no sense of decency, sir?"

McCarthy lost his composure and was seen on television as a tyrant. The press leaped on the chance to show McCarthy, the unscrupulous bully, and Welch, the indignant and honest gentleman, face to face. The subcommittee cleared the army of McCarthy's charges. His reputation crumbled, and his political backers abandoned him.

A Mighty Nation and Nonconformity

Despite the fear of communism, most Americans could feel confident in their nation's strength and its future prosperity. Easygoing, grandfatherly President Eisenhower symbolized what mainstream Americans felt about their country. Many saw his relaxed style and modesty as examples for their own lives.

Although Republicans held the White House, Democrats had the majority in the House of Representatives and Senate at the end of the decade.

Many people became tired of the paranoia about the Cold War and "the bomb." "Live for today" became a recurring new theme in people's lives, especially young people. As the 1950s closed, they wanted to shake off the constant anxiety they had known all their lives. They longed to celebrate and enjoy a prosperous and powerful America.

In these decades, feminism was less influential than in previous generations. At the same time, women were changing, and new ideas were taking hold. Planned Parenthood was founded in 1948 to offer advice on birth control, although abortion remained illegal. Abortions took place in spite of the law, but they were often dangerous for the pregnant female. Anyone performing abortions faced severe punishment and prison if arrested and found guilty.

Although women were still portrayed either as sex objects or as motherly, they were also seen as having minds of their own, separate from men. In film and magazines, sexuality became more free and easy. At the same time, many women took pride in being independent thinkers who could take charge of their own bodies.

There was a trend toward conformity throughout the 1950s. There was also a powerful counterforce at work. Art became

Poet Allen Ginsberg was one of the main figures of the Beatnik generation of the late 1950s. Together with fellow writers such as Jack Kerouac, Gregory Corso, and Lawrence Ferlinghetti, Ginsberg represented a rejection of 1950s conformity. (Library of Congress)

more abstract and free-form than ever before, as did music. Jazz and traditional folk music combined to appeal to a segment of youth culture known as the Beats, or Beatniks.

At the heart of Beat culture was disillusionment with the American dream of a suburban home and a two-car garage. Beatniks believed this dream was shallow, empty. They took the name Beat because they felt that society had beaten down their own hopes for a better world. Beat culture flourished in coffee-houses and cafés. There, jazz and poetry performances intermingled with old socialist songs of workers' rights and human freedom. The "Beat Generation's" notions of personal freedom and rebellion against established culture were spread by their writings. Among the best known figures in Beat culture were novelist Jack Kerouac, author of On the Road, and poet Allen Ginsberg, who's best known poem was "Howl."

By the end of the 1950s, the Beat culture had been discovered and publicized by the press and television. Its writers and thinkers became familiar names, although they symbolized unconventional morality and lack of ambition. The Beats laid the foundation for the next decade's rebels who would create a counterculture that would become firmly established in the American mainstream.

The Era's Closing Election

With the 1960 presidential election came widespread television coverage of the candidates' debates. Eisenhower's vice president, Richard M. Nixon of California, ran against Massachusetts senator John F. Kennedy for the Democrats.

Nixon symbolized the established order of things, while Kennedy was the newcomer, handsome and charming. Though his television presence was already commanding, Kennedy used makeup skillfully to compensate for the harshness of stage lighting. Kennedy came across as fresh, while Nixon looked tired, in need of a good shave.

Kennedy won the election by only 118,550 popular votes in a total of 86.3 million cast. It was, until then, the closest presidential election of the century. That Kennedy was Catholic was proof of a change in American thinking. Previously, only Protestants had been president. Also, at 43, he was the youngest president ever elected.

Chapter Three

Education

Before the 1940s, a high-school diploma was highly respected, but few people were able to get one. It was mainly children from well-to-do families who completed high school, called "secondary school." By 1940, however, that had changed, as 1.2 million students graduated, compared to 667,000 in 1930.

Despite the high-school population boom, the number of students in college grew more slowly at the start of the decade. In 1940, 186,000 people graduated from college, compared to 122,000 in 1930. When World War II ended in 1945 however, everything changed again. Thanks to federal government programs for former soldiers and sailors, college attendance soared. The government paid the tuition of more than 2.2 million war veterans. In 1950, more than 432,000 students earned college diplomas.

College-level education became a major business between 1940 and 1960. Before this time, most colleges were private. Now great public–university systems were growing fast. Not only four-year schools developed, but two-year colleges also began to appear. For whites, a high school diploma became less valuable. It was a college degree that counted most. African Americans still struggled to get even the most basic education. Those who attended college and graduate school usually enrolled in institutions founded for African Americans.

Segregated educational systems resulted in poor schools, or

Students at Beloit College (LEFT) **in Wisconsin in the early 1950s turn in their exams to their professor.** (Courtesy Beloit College Archive) **Elementary school students in New York City** (RIGHT) **raise their hands.** (Hulton Getty Archive)

none at all, for black children. Black students were kept out of most colleges, either because of segregation or because they had not been given a fair educational opportunity. The growing Civil Rights movement aimed at opening every level of the American educational system to blacks. As secondary and higher education grew in the United States, the Civil Rights movement also grew. In 1954, the Supreme Court declared segregated schools to be against the Constitution. Most educational institutions were slow to desegregate. Still, by 1960 black students were being admitted to schools and colleges that once had barred them. There was much more to be done to overcome racial segregation, but the foundation for change was firmly established.

During these years, many educators believed that American schools were falling behind the rest of the world. The dangers of the Cold War made Americans fear that Russia would get ahead of them. Competition between the two countries was not only military but also in the race to put a satellite into orbit around the earth. This was the "Space Race," and Russia seemed to be winning.

Teenagers Appear on the Scene

In the 1940s, something new was happening to young people. Before this time, they were considered to be like adults. They dressed and behaved like adults and went out to work. With the growth in high-school enrollment, that changed. Now large numbers of young people spent most of their day together, in school.

The halls of secondary education were open to millions more young Americans, and they created a world of their own. This age group took on its own identity and first became known as "teenagers." They dressed in their own fashions, not like adults. Girls wore low socks, called bobby socks, shorter skirts, and saddle shoes. Boys wore leather jackets and blue jeans. Teenagers enjoyed being together, separate from their elders.

By the 1950s, the identity of teenagers was firmly established. Advertising and business took the opportunity to sell the products and goods teenagers wanted. This created a powerful culture with new tastes in movies, cars, and clothes. Teens even began to dance to rhythm and blues, a traditional music of African Americans, instead of the popular swing music of the 1930s and early 1940s. While their elders were chasing the dream of a good home and job, the teenagers of the late 1940s and 1950s became a new social group.

Many parents were troubled by the behavior of their children. Parents did not understand why teenagers wanted to be different. More than any generation before them, young people were looking to each other for new ideas and styles.

School Sports

The high school's social life was what interested students most of all. Students gathered in the halls or on the playgrounds and in after-school programs. "Scholastic sports," as school athletics were known, was the most important of all.

Most scholastic athletes were male in these years, because girls' sports were few and far between. Instead, girls were cheerleaders, flag swingers, and marching band members. Toward the end of the 1950s, more and more girls' sports programs were being organized. Educators and parents worried, however, that girls would not be able to compete as vigorously as boys. Girls were thought to be vulnerable to injury if they tried too hard, ran too fast, or became too excited. Yet girls' sports grew steadily, especially basketball, softball, and field hockey.

Members of the basketball team at Lafayette High School, Brooklyn, New York, line up to practice shooting from the foul line. (Archives Photos)

The Chrome-Yellow School Bus

Across America in the early 1940s, school-children were being transported in all sorts of vehicles. These ranged from horse-drawn carts and motorized hay wagons to family cars and the latest school buses.

Like the carts and wagons, school buses came in many different sizes and designs. Now that was changing. New national standards for school-bus design, construction, and even color were being put into effect. In the 1940s, the first official yellow school buses began to operate.

Some wealthy school districts had used motorized school buses for at least twenty-five years. Other districts had found the buses just too expensive to buy. Since every state had designed its own buses, the manufacturers had been unable to mass produce one cost-efficient design. In 1939, educators, state transportation officials, and bus manufacturers finally agreed on design and construction.

From then on, buses were built with the same construction standards. Some manufacturers specialized in making specific standard parts, such as chassis, wheels, or engines. This brought costs down, and school districts across the nation could afford buses.

Officials also chose a color, which they called "National School Bus Chrome." Before school-bus yellow became standard, buses had been painted a wide variety of colors. Some were purple, others green or red. One district in New York painted buses with patriotic red, white, and blue stripes. For safety reasons, it was important that school buses be highly visible, since they made so many stops. Chrome yellow was the best choice because it stood out in dim light and in rain and fog.

The new school bus standards were accepted in most states by 1950. School-bus yellow was seen almost everywhere. Minnesota, however, created its own color: "Minnesota Golden Orange." It would not be until 1974 that Minnesota changed to the standard chrome yellow.

Running for the school bus in Salinas, California, in the early 1940s. (National Archives)

Scholastic sports were considered an important part of the student's learning experience. A student benefited from being on a team, playing according to the rules, learning teamwork and self-sacrifice. In most small towns, the high-school football or basketball team was the pride of the community. Everyone went to the big games, and star athletes were the most-admired local heroes.

By the 1940s and 1950s, state athletic associations had been formed to govern school sports. Teams were organized into leagues, and safety was of prime importance. Coaches were required to take basic courses to prepare for handling young athletes. Competition between rival high schools could be ferocious, but at least it was kept under control by trained referees and league officials.

Poor students who might otherwise have dropped out of high school often stayed in because they took part in athletics. Most states began to adopt regulations that required athletes to have minimum classroom grades to compete. As more and more students wanted to participate in athletics, additional sports were added. By the end of the 1950s, athletics were the main focus of student life in most American high schools.

Preparing for College or Work

Since the 1920s, high schools had offered increasingly different education to different students. College-bound students concentrated on grammar, history, mathematics, science, languages, and American literature. Those who were not going on to college were taught subjects that prepared them for work—that is, for their "vocations." Boys learned the skilled trades, and girls studied business skills. The boys were taught "manual arts," such as mechanics, wood and metal shop, and working with tools. The girls took a "commercial," or secretarial, course and learned bookkeeping, typing, filing, and stenography skills. Vocational students took only the most basic courses in English, social studies, and arithmetic. There was also a "general" course, which mixed academic and commercial courses.

Some critics complained that the standards of American education were falling steadily. With so many students in high school, the courses were being made too easy. They strongly objected to high schools teaching "life-adjustment education" courses. Since 1918, the National Education Association had argued that high schools should educate students socially as well as academically and vocationally. These skills included how to care for one's appearance, dating, and healthy boy-girl relationships. Others were education in citizenship, in home and family life, and how best to use leisure time. "Life-adjustment courses" also taught personal health, about the importance of getting work experience, and how to fit into society.

Many educators and parents worried that a solid academic education or vocational training were not being stressed enough. Americans generally believed mathematics and science instruction were falling short of what was needed. By the late 1950s, it seemed schools were failing.

Sputnik Shocks America

In October 1957, the Russians launched *Sputnik I*, the first satellite to orbit the earth. American scientists were surprised to be left behind, and so was the government. Some people became concerned that the rest of the world would believe communism was superior to democracy. Others were concerned that the Russians would leave the United States even further behind in the race for space, which aimed at one day putting a person on the moon.

Sputnik was about the size of a basketball and went around the earth once every ninety-six minutes. Each time it made another journey, it seemed America was falling farther and farther behind in the space race. The federal government and Congress decided to pour money into education, especially into science and math. The result was the National Defense Education Act of 1958, which made available $47.5 million in student loans. That amount would grow every year, with more than $100 million being loaned annually by the early 1960s. These loans were mainly for studying science, engineering, or foreign languages. Over the next four years, the government also made nearly $300 million available to purchase scientific equipment and for grants to graduate students.

As never before, federal funds supported and promoted American education at every level. Colleges and universities established new departments to meet the requirements of the space race. Public education also changed in this time.

Teachers and Teaching

During World War II, so many young adults were away at war that there was a severe shortage of teachers. Salaries were low, and for that reason large numbers of teachers left the profession. They took higher-paying jobs in business and industry.

After the war, thousands of returning service personnel were looking for work. They often wanted to become teachers, but that was becoming difficult to do. First, there were not enough teaching positions available. Second, states now were requiring more training for teachers. Many older teachers did not have college degrees, but new teachers were expected to have their diplomas. School boards were raising the basic requirements for a teaching license, and more teacher colleges were established.

Most teachers were women. In 1940, only one teacher in five was male. As the profession became better paid, more men began to enter it. Because the men often had advanced college or university degrees, they generally taught in the higher grades. Elementary school teachers continued to be mainly women.

Early in this period, female teachers were still expected to be unmarried. Once they did marry, they usually left the profession to care for their families. By the mid-1950s that was changing. Because of the baby boom, there was a great need for teachers. At the same time, many married women wanted to go back to work. Married women were hired as teachers in large numbers. This broke the longstanding custom of hiring only unmarried women as teachers.

Other important changes were taking place in the teaching profession. By the mid-1940s, teachers were organizing into a national union. As the years passed, they demanded better pay, more benefits, and improved working conditions. At this time, teachers first began to go on strike, and the public was shocked. Eventually, however, teachers' unions won rights, higher salaries, and respect for the profession.

City Schools and Discipline

In schools all across the United States, the day began with a morning prayer, a reading from the Bible, and the Pledge of Allegiance. Whether it was a one-room school in Montana or a crowded inner-city school on the East Coast, these same rituals were followed. The rest of the school day was very different, however.

Students recite the Pledge of Allegiance in Los Angeles, California in the 1940s. (Library of Congress)

Often, parents and teachers cooperated to get their children the best educations possible. Most parents also helped to keep their children disciplined. In the cities, though, student discipline could be difficult to maintain. Parents were often too busy or too poor to help with their children's education. Or, perhaps, the only parent was a working mother struggling to feed her family. Many inner-city children did not live with their own parents. As a result, there was no real support for them from home.

In cities like New York, the population was rapidly changing. Neighborhoods that once had been all Italian or Irish were becoming all Puerto Rican or African American. Many children in these neighborhoods lived with aunts and uncles or older brothers and sisters instead of with their parents. African American families from the South often sent their children to the northern cities. In the North, the education and opportunities were far better. It was the same for many Puerto Rican children, who were sent to New York for a better life. Without having parents on hand, however, these children could be difficult to teach.

For those children who had no supervision at home, street gangs often were their families. Life was violent for them almost every day. The most determined of these children worked hard and were successful at getting an education. Others were sent to city vocational schools to learn a trade. For many inner-city children, however, school ended by age fifteen, when they quit to go to work. In time, they would be drafted into the military or would enlist in the service of their choice. Education was also available in the military. Young people often came out of the service with skills that helped them to get jobs. But too many inner-city children of high-school age became juvenile delinquents and were put in reform school or prison.

A heavy burden fell on the city-school teachers to maintain discipline and also educate the children. City schools in these years often had excellent, dedicated teachers and administrators. Administrators and teaching staff often made sure to get shoes or coats for the poorest children. The funds generally came from private donations or were provided by the teachers themselves.

Public schools in the city varied widely in quality. Yet many cities had one or two special high schools that took in only the best, most talented students. They took in students from all walks of life and did not discriminate by race or religion. These schools offered a first-rate academic education as well as courses in art, drama, and music. In some such schools, students were especially good in science and math. In northern cities, these high schools made it possible for students of all races and social classes to go on to higher education.

Segregation and Separation

In the South and in border states such as Kansas, West Virginia, and Missouri, public schools were segregated by race, either as all-white or all-black schools. While there was plenty of poverty among southern whites, their poorest schools seemed rich compared to the standard black schools. Many black schools could not even afford to hire janitorial staff. Children and teachers had to clean the schools themselves. Their textbooks were old and worn, if there were any at all. The building was often unheated, and children could not afford even pencils and paper. In southern white schools, athletes had excellent equipment, athletic fields, and gymnasiums. Black athletes in black schools had

In 1957, nine Little Rock, Arkansas, students helped desegregate the city's Central High School. They are seen here with Daisy Bates (BACK, SECOND FROM RIGHT), a civil rights worker with the National Association for the Advancement of Colored People. (Library of Congress)

almost nothing at all in the way of facilities and equipment.

Conditions in white and black schools in the South were completely unequal in regard to education, facilities, and opportunity. Even the teachers in black schools were paid far less than those in white schools. Many black communities in the South had no high schools at all.

In the North, many schools were unofficially segregated because students mainly came from an all-white or all-black neighborhood. As in the South, this separation of the races also resulted in black schools being less prosperous than white schools.

A major change in American education occurred in 1954. That year, the U.S. Supreme Court announced a decision that shook up the nation. The case was brought by an African American minister in Topeka, Kansas, who demanded that his little daughter be admitted to an all-white school. The decision in the case, *Brown v. Board of Education of Topeka,* declared that racial segregation in public schools was unconstitutional. The Court said the Constitution requires that every citizen have equal rights under the law. Since segregated public schools were unequal, that meant black students were being denied their constitutional rights. Segregation in public education was required to come to an end.

Desegregation of schools would move very slowly. In the meantime, the struggle for civil rights in education went on. One of the worst conflicts took place in Little Rock, Arkansas, in 1957. Segregationists armed themselves to prevent integration of schools. President Eisenhower believed that the Supreme Court had to be obeyed, whether people liked it or not. He sent in troops to enforce the law, and there was a fierce battle before peace returned to the city.

One important result of the Little Rock conflict was that the federal government had stepped in on the side of integration. More than ever before, the power of the national government was on the side of those working for civil rights.

The Cutback in Vocational Education

Vocational schools and education represented another kind of segregation. This was segregation by social class. Vocational students were usually from poorer families. They were considered unable to learn as well as college-preparatory students could learn. While students were training to become blue-collar workers, they did not get a good general education. This created a deep divide between the students in a school. Some were college-bound, others were work-bound.

"Techs" were mostly for boys. Now, instead of being part of a high-school student body, vocational pupils were separated even further from other children. Often it was the problem students who were sent to technical schools. If a pupil caused trouble in a high school, or if he had problems learning, he was often sent to technical school. This seemed more like a punishment than a way to learn.

Late in the 1950s, educators began to consider "difficult" students in a new way. More and more, educators came to realize that moving them into vocational programs did not help them. The rise in juvenile crime year after year proved this. These

A student at Brooklyn School of Automotive Trades, in Brooklyn, New York.
(Hulton Archives)

children often saw no future for themselves. As a result, they often became involved in alcohol, drugs, and crime. Making things worse, manual-arts jobs were becoming harder for a vocational student to find. American industry was fast-changing, using new production methods and equipment, but vocational education was not keeping up with that change.

Educators came to believe in giving these students a general education instead of vocational training. Many vocational programs were being abandoned. The same would eventually happen to vocational high schools.

Private and Parochial Schools

At the start of the 1940s, private schools were much like private colleges. Sometimes called "independent" schools, they were expensive and exclusive. Their students were from wealthier families and were being groomed to enter the best universities. Peaceful, private campuses and beautiful surroundings gave these schools an atmosphere of superiority.

What was sorely lacking in wealthy private schools was diversity in student body and the staff. Most private schools admitted either all boys or all girls. Almost everyone was white and Protestant. These schools were described as "walled-in gardens." By the late 1950s, American society was changing. In part because of the Civil Rights movement, races and religions were beginning to mingle as never before. As a result, many private-school administrators realized that their students should learn to take part in those changes. Student bodies and teaching staff began to include persons from other religions and races and from lower economic levels. Students received more well-rounded educations.

Catholic, or parochial, schools were also private. A few were as exclusive as private independent schools, but most were like public schools. One difference was that religious instruction was part of the curriculum, so these schools attracted mainly Catholic children. Most teachers were also Catholic, and many were nuns. Their instruction was usually better than the average public school, and discipline was stricter. While public-school teachers were not allowed to strike troublesome students, Catholic-school teachers could and often did.

Many new parochial schools were built in the suburbs, where

Catholic families were moving. With the departure of these families from the cities, the older parochial schools struggled for funds. Most city Catholic schools continued to serve their changing communities throughout the 1950s. Loyalty to them remained strong in the new generation of parents and children.

Special Education

No students of this period were so overlooked as those with mental or physical handicaps. Such children usually had been kept at home, hidden away. There were some private schools for the mentally disabled and handicapped, but almost nothing was available for them in public schools.

For example, children in wheelchairs would be turned away from enrolling in public schools. Often they were excellent students, but their disability kept them out of public school. They had to be tutored at home, or they attended schools for the blind, deaf, or orthopedically disabled—"crippled children."

Parents of mentally and physically handicapped children were inspired by activists who were fighting racial segregation. Joining with allies in the teaching profession, these parents worked to make a place for their children in public schools. "Special education" began to take shape. Too often such children were put in a classroom in the basement of the school, far from the rest of the students. In time, however, that began to change. "Special" children received better care. They came in contact more often with other children during the school day, if only passing in the halls.

Then, in 1958, the first federal law regarding special education was passed. The Education of Mentally Retarded Children Act made funding available to train teachers for special-education programs. A new era in educating the handicapped now began.

Chapter Four

The Economy

The food section of a supermarket in Yonkers, New York in 1954 (LEFT); (Archive Photos) shopping day in Putnam County, Georgia in 1941 (RIGHT). (National Archives)

The hard economic times of the 1930s ended when the United States again prepared for war in the 1940s. The Great Depression and its millions of unemployed abruptly gave way to full employment. There was even plenty of work for women and teenagers.

During World War II, there was not much to purchase when workers got their weekly paycheck. Most of what the country produced went to the military in these years. Car production was stopped in 1942 so that military vehicles and equipment could be built instead. In the middle of the war, the government froze prices and wages to prevent inflation. What goods and products did exist for the consumer to buy were strictly rationed. All this changed swiftly after the war ended in 1945.

Much of the industrialized world lay in ruins. But America was not damaged by the war. Factories were humming, and consumer goods soon began to appear in the stores again. Americans were eager to spend the money they had saved during the frugal wartime years. Spending skyrocketed on new consumer goods. Although there were economic downturns from time to time, the American economy roared through the 1940s and 1950s. These boom times were fueled by consumer demand for housing, automobiles, and modern household appliances.

Foreign trade was also strong, as American products found ready buyers around the world. Europe recovered its own production capacity by the late 1950s and became less dependent on American products. Still, the United States had the latest styles and most modern appliances. It was also the greatest producer of food in the world. American farmers were astonishingly productive, and food prices were low. Agriculture was increasingly dominated by huge corporations that kept prices and costs low. The result was that family farms could not compete. Their numbers began a steady decline.

Some manufacturing competition appeared in Japan and Hong Kong and in other Asian countries in the 1950s. These were often cheaply made toys, housewares, and clothing. The quality was poor at first. That would change by 1960, as Asian manufacturers began to produce goods that were not only cheap to purchase but of excellent quality.

Shopping was essential to the lives of most American families. In 1939, retailers had persuaded President Roosevelt to move Thanksgiving closer to the Christmas shopping season. The holiday tradition of furiously shopping for presents between Thanksgiving and Christmas became firmly established.

At first it seemed like the economy could keep on growing forever. Some thought it must go on growing, year after year, to maintain the modern lifestyle. Yet the nation entered the 1960s with a changing attitude toward consumption. For one thing, there was a growing movement, backed by the

A woman uses a "ration book" to purchase sugar during World War II (LEFT); a gasoline ration stamp (ABOVE). (Library of Congress)

1958: A Remarkable Year for Consumers

The year 1958 was notable for some consumer-oriented milestones. The postage stamp went up to four cents for a first-class letter. This was the first rise in cost for twenty-six years. Also this year, the credit cards VISA and MasterCard were introduced. The new Boeing 707 passenger airliner offered larger passenger capacity and promised cheaper airfares. The new artificial sweetener Sweet 'n' Low used saccharin instead of sugar. Also in this year, Cocoa Puffs cereal appeared. Unlike Sweet 'n' Low, Cocoa Puffs were 43 percent sugar. In addition, the first Pizza Hut opened in Kansas City, establishing another chain of fast-food restaurants.

Inside the hula-hoop factory. (Courtesy of Wham-O, Inc.)

Yet, it was not air travel or credit cards or fast food that won the hearts of Americans in 1958. It was the Hula Hoop. Produced by the Wham-O company, Hula Hoops were an immediate sensation. Before long, more than 100 million colorful hoops were whirling around American hips, arms, legs, and necks. The Wham-O company had brought out another plaything in 1957, but its time had not yet come. It was called the Frisbee.

federal government, to make sure products were safe and did what they claimed. For another, some critics believed "mindless consumption" was spoiling the children. Having so many material things was causing Americans to become incredibly wasteful. Pollution of water and air and the devouring of natural resources were proof of that.

The Advertising Message: Buy

To keep Americans consuming, the advertising industry enthusiastically encouraged the nation to buy as much as possible. Ample credit was available from the banks and from the department stores themselves. "Buy now, pay later," was the theme of the day.

Makers of consumer goods, products, services, and producers of entertainment got their messages to consumers by placing ads in publications and in the broadcast media. Advertising in magazines, newspapers, and on the radio promoted the latest model of cars and the brand of cigarettes that "doctors recommend most." (Cigarettes were not declared unhealthy until 1964.) When televisions appeared in almost every home, commercial images dominated much of American home life.

The most important target for many of these ads was young people. For one thing, children who were familiar with a product would continue to buy it when they grew up. There were other important reasons to sell to children. New fashions, electronic gadgets, processed foods, and music styles were changing fast. The avalanche of new products sometimes confused adults, but young people were eagerly staying up-to-date with the latest developments and products. By 1948, there was even whipped cream in an aerosol can.

Magazines for teens only and teen-advice columns in newspapers appeared in the mid-1940s. *Seventeen* magazine was founded in 1944, with fashion news and advice for girls about their problems. The magazine also tried to offer educational value. One issue even had an article explaining atomic power. Readers complained, though. Instead, they wanted movie stars, advice on dating, and more pages on fashion. Young people now were mighty consumers, and becoming mightier. A manufacturer sold $12 million worth of girls' dresses just from 1944 to 1946.

The rise of television in the mid-1950s gave advertisers the greatest marketing medium ever. Americans enjoyed broadcast entertainment in their own homes. First they had listened to the radio, later they sat in front of the television. Then they loved TV dinners, which could be kept frozen in the modern, new refrigerator and quickly heated in the modern, all-electric oven. Processed food could be frozen as well as canned, and frozen was said to be "fresher." Plastic Tupperware, plastic wrap, and aluminum foil took care of the leftovers, which were placed back in the refrigerator. Plastic kitchen goods were conveniences that no depression-era homemaker ever knew.

An early advertisement for Swanson TV Dinner.
(Courtesy of Swanson, Inc.)

Advertisements displayed products in settings that often depicted the rich in elegant mansions, on yachts, with fast cars, or wearing precious jewelry and fine clothes. Ads stimulated the viewer's appetite for the product and the world surrounding it. This took advantage of people's longing to possess, and also their burning envy. For example, the Hoover vacuum cleaner company showed well-to-do women using their vacuums. The average housewife who saw that commercial wanted to be like the wealthy ladies. The housewife could not help imagining having a Hoover of her own.

The Hoover company knew ordinary people liked the idea of having appliances that were used by the very rich. In fact, many housewives could afford to buy a Hoover on credit. Hoover was one of the most successful vacuum cleaners in the world during these decades. Millions of housewives saw Hoover television commercials on their favorite television shows. Those housewives were well prepared for a Hoover salesman to appear at the door.

The rest of the world began to watch television, too, and saw America's bounding prosperity. American products were favored in other countries, and American styles in clothing and music were widely copied. Few countries had the room for sprawling suburbs, however, with single-family homes and one or two cars in the driveway. The rest of the world longed for this kind of prosperity. They admired what was known as the "American way of life." Foreigners wanted to have the latest American-style household gadgets. They wanted to "live like an American."

Supermarkets, Malls, and Dolls

The suburbs, with its prosperity and its automobile culture, were the natural habitat for consumers. It was costly to maintain the house and lawn, to get and care for the late-model car, and to buy the best television before the neighbor did. There was little in the way of mass transit to and from the suburbs. Travel had to be by car. A gallon of gasoline cost almost twenty cents in the mid-1940s, when per-capita income was less than $1,200 a year.

Shoppers from suburbs and towns drove out to large, new supermarkets and department stores that anchored the many strip malls being built on suburban highways. The department stores of the early twentieth century had been lavish and enticing. They brought women and girls downtown to shop in attractive,

pleasing surroundings. This changed with the rise of suburban malls. Modern supermarkets offered brisk efficiency, lots of parking, standardized foods, and products packaged to appeal to modern tastes. And their prices were much cheaper than the family-run, neighborhood grocery stores. The neighborhood grocery was vanishing.

The restaurant business was also challenged. In 1955, the nation's first McDonald's hamburger franchise opened in Des Plaines, Illinois. Burgers were fifteen cents and fries cost five cents. It was difficult for a sit-down restaurant to compete with new businesses that offered convenient, fast food eaten on the run. Customers did not even have to leave their cars to place an order and eat. There always had been cheap "hamburger stands" in city neighborhoods, but McDonald's set its sights on the suburbs. It appealed to busy shoppers who did not want to sit down and wait for food preparation. People seemed to have less patience during these days, and no time to relax.

As the suburbs spread farther and farther from the city, people became isolated in their homes with their televisions. Seventeen thousand sets were in use in 1946, but they had tiny, five-inch black-and-white screens. Still, television was more exciting than radio, and the screen was getting better all the time. Seven years later, there were 7 millions sets. In 1954, the first color televisions came on the market. By the 1960s, there were 90 million televisions in the United States.

As early as the mid-1950s, children spent more hours at home watching television than in school. The shows and advertising influenced young viewers powerfully. They wanted to be like the stars, to talk and dress like them and to live as they lived. Children also wanted what they saw on the commercials. To these, America's youngest consumers, the ideal images on television seemed like real life.

For many young girls, their ideal was to be found in a new doll that appeared for the first time in 1959, "Barbie." A blonde teenager with a perfect figure and long legs, Barbie was a rebel in her own way. Most other dolls were cuddly and cute, but Barbie was like an imaginary older sister. She had an entire wardrobe, including glamorous designer outfits and strapless swimsuits. And Barbie could be kept in style from year to year, with the latest fashion. She even had her own sports car. To many young girls, Barbie was the ideal girl. She was also a runaway success from the start.

The original Barbie, from 1959. (Courtesy of Mattel, Inc.)

Keeping Up with the Joneses

Amid all the prosperity, social critics charged that Americans were much too wasteful. Some believed American companies were making products no one really needed and throwing things away before they were used.

Previous generations had been thrifty. They kept things until they wore out. Americans were now so prosperous that it was normal to buy the latest model and eliminate the one that was out of date. Toasters, radios, televisions, and vacuums might be thrown away even if they still worked. Families showed off their financial success by trading in their cars and buying a new one every year—or by buying a second car.

There was increasing concern that the most important aspect of American life was ever-growing consumption. Young people, it was said, were so swamped in material goods that they were becoming spoiled. Indeed, for many people, being a consumer was what mattered most. They were identified by what they owned and what they could buy. Other than watching television, shopping was becoming the main leisure activity for millions of Americans.

Yet by the late 1950s, more and more Americans were questioning their culture's unending drive to spend and consume. They objected to the obsession of having a better home or car than the neighbors. This buying in order to look wealthy or to seem up-to-date was termed *conspicuous consumption*. This term meant buying products that were intended to be shown off. It also meant buying too much, such as foodstuffs, and being wasteful.

Certainly businesses wanted American consumers to buy more of everything every year. One leading designer of appliances said the economy depended on new merchandise quickly becoming old-fashioned or out of style. Of course, many items had been intentionally made to fall apart in a short time. In this way, they had to be replaced, so the buying cycle continued.

"Keeping up with the Joneses" was and expression describing families who struggled to look as prosperous or modern as their neighbors. This race for material things included new cars, clothing, household goods, and appliances. It also included the beauty of the front lawn and the quality of the lawn mower. Late in the 1950s, families competed to take the most exciting vacations by airplanes to distant places. Also compared were the children's college educations and whose college had more prestige.

Since all this was expensive, Americans got into debt as never before in history. While the Great Depression had turned many people against borrowing, the culture of the 1940s and 1950s made it easy to go into debt. To keep up with the Joneses, there was no choice but to borrow.

Conformity, Rebellion, and Wheels

By the early 1950s, most World War II veterans and their wives had settled into predictable lives. The men usually had good jobs and the women were raising families. What middle-class families wanted most was the opportunity for the man to "climb the corporate ladder" to become even better-off.

To achieve the American dream of prosperity often required fitting into society's generally accepted idea of lifestyles. For the businessman to succeed, for example, he had to look like the others in his world. He dressed conservatively, perhaps in a gray flannel suit and fedora hat. He bought a good house in the right neighborhood. He sent his kids to the right schools. He did not draw attention at work but did his job efficiently and quietly. This was the "organization man."

In 1955, author Sloan Wilson published a novel about the conflict between family values and an organization man's ambition, called *The Man in the Gray-Flannel Suit*. The book became a best-seller, and the following year it was made into a popular movie. Many American families saw themselves and their own lives in the story.

The mood of the generation that fought World War II was defined by conformity and patriotism. Yet certain politicians beat the drum of fear, warning of communist spies in government. The Cold War had settled down over a world divided, East and West, characterized by fear and suspicion. In the United States, with its own problems of racial segregation and inequality, people could do best economically if they fit into the system. Then they would be able to satisfy their personal needs and desires by shopping, consuming. Mass production of goods and products readily kept up with consumer demand. Through the 1950s, there was employment and prosperity for much of the nation. With the world's worries hanging over Americans, shopping continued as a favorite pastime for many.

Although most adults had settled down, thousands of young people raced around the countryside on their Harley-Davidsons. This popular motorcycle had been used widely by the military during the war. Riders seemed to resist the conformity of the men in gray flannel suits. Through the 1950s, films and television portrayed bikers as rebels against society. That image took hold as actors such as Marlon Brando and James Dean played angry young men who objected to the consumer culture. They were hostile to the values of that society. The motorcycle crowd might be fashioned after media stars, but they were not rock-solid consumers like suburbanites. Many bikers were, instead, part of a growing "counterculture" that opposed mindless consumption.

Meanwhile, quiet, hard-working parents pursued their passion for the latest model car or washing machine. American manufacturing knew what they wanted and gave it to them. In 1951, the family camera was fitted with a built-in flash, so indoor pho-

A father and son wash the family's Ford Fairlane automobile in the driveway of their home. (Archive Photos)

tography became easy and popular. The next year, area codes were developed to handle the millions of new telephones that were now in homes.

The automobile, more than any consumer product, was what best identified consumers. What cars people drove told much about who they were. In the 1950s, many Americans were attracted to a new wave of European "sports cars." German and British manufacturers were recovering well from the war, and sports cars like the British two-seater MG appealed to young people. Still, the average American drove a big, roomy Ford or Chevrolet in the 1950s. Family outings were by car, and the station wagon became popular. This model was designed for families and pets and picnic gear all to be packed into the back.

As the automobile culture exploded in these years, the road system kept up with it. Throughout the 1950s, the federal government was busy linking major cities with 42,500 miles of new highways. This construction was authorized by the Federal Highway Act passed by Congress in 1956. That same year, the first seat belts appeared. They were one of the few safety items incorporated into automobile design, but they were not standard equipment. American cars were built for speed, comfort, and good looks—not safety—and they consumed large quantities of gasoline. Few American drivers cared about gas mileage, because gas stayed cheap, and cash was plentiful.

Although annual deaths in autos were in the 40,000 range, manufacturers did not want to raise costs by redesigning cars for safety. Anyway, consumers seemed to care more about the bumper's shiny chrome or the sweep of the rear "fins" than whether the car would hold up in a crash. Consumers did not want to spend more for automotive safety, either.

The major American auto manufacturers were sure they knew what the consumer wanted in a car. They were not always right. In 1957, Ford Motor Company learned this bitter lesson. The company released the Edsel, a large and boxy passenger car. It had rakish tail fins and an unusual front grille, shaped like a combination oval and rectangle. Some described it as a horse collar. The Edsel was named for Edsel Ford, the son of founder Henry Ford. The company launched the model with a massive $250 million advertising campaign. It was not enough. The Edsel was a failure. Within a couple of years after its introduction, Ford's newest model was canceled, after about 118,000 were built.

One reason the Edsel failed was problems in manufacturing that caused mechanical difficulties. Also, the Edsel was a huge gas-guzzler. The public was thinking finally about smaller, more efficient cars. Ford's sporty Thunderbird and the modest Rambler American, both smaller cars, were successful in this time.

An advertisement for the Ford Edsel (TOP) and a far more successful Ford Thunderbird (BOTTOM). (Library of Congress)

The VW Bug Arrives

At the same time, another segment of the consumer market was beginning to rebel against both conspicuous consumption and big, expensive cars. They wanted a car that was cheap and efficient with gasoline. This car would make a statement that its owner opposed conformity and also was a pioneer in a new way of driving and thinking. The car that met these needs was

Volkswagen Beetles were first introduced to the United States in 1949. The original model remained in production for more than half a century. (Archive Photos)

the German-made Volkswagen Beetle.

Since being introduced to the United States in 1949, the Volkswagen had steadily increased its share of the automotive market. Between 1955-1958, foreign-made small cars made a strong showing in sales. Their share rose from 0.5 percent of the American market to 8 percent. Half of those foreign cars were Volkswagens. College students were among the most enthusiastic owners of Beetles, or "Bugs," as they were also called. This little car did not have much room, its engine was tiny, and its design did not change from year to year. Because the engine was in the back, Beetles were unsafe in head-on collisions. The VW Beetle did have an aura of being different, however, of being an alternative to the gas-guzzlers.

This aura did not just happen. The image came to be thanks to an advertising program that had gained powerful momentum by 1960. The VW Bug was positioned as a symbol of counter-culture thinking. The manufacturer agreed in the ads that the Beetle was ugly. But it was built to last, not to be out of date in a year or two. Unlike American cars, the Beetle was contrary to conspicuous consumption, and its owners made that statement clearly each time they drove the Bug.

It would take time for American cars to become smaller—"compact," they would be called in the 1960s. Yet the VW Beetle had found its place in American culture, and the major auto manufacturers took notice.

Advertising and the New Counterculture

By 1960, the spirit of rebelling against accepted norms and traditions was a theme of national advertising. Instead of conforming to an image, Americans were encouraged to be more independent thinkers,—free spirits. Products and services were advertised as being hip and avant-garde (French for "advance guard," or "cutting-edge"). Mass-market advertising encouraged the fledgling counterculture to "think young" and be different. Of course, they should continue faithfully buying what was advertised on television and depicted in the movies.

Throughout much of this era, it seemed the nation's natural resources were endless. Gasoline was fairly cheap in 1960, costing thirty-one cents a gallon, while per-capita income was approximately $2,200 annually. There were abundant forests, unmined mountains of minerals and coal, untapped oil fields, natural gas, and all the water needed for drinking and for irrigating farm fields. The entire nation was being "electrified," with new power generators and dams, and power lines that stretched from Niagara Falls to New York City. In 1959, one of the nation's earliest nuclear-powered, electric generating plants went into operation in Illinois. At first it was believed that nuclear power would do away with pollution and with fossil fuels. By the close of the 1950s, however, the urge toward independent thinking helped make people reconsider what was happening all around them.

Water and air pollution could not be ignored much longer. In the rush to produce and to consume, the nation was fouling its rivers, creating a blanket of smog over its cities, and clear-cutting its forests. The population had grown from 131.6 million in 1940 to 179.3 million in 1960. Even the suburbs were beginning to feel overcrowded and congested with traffic. Endless economic growth could go on only so long. For the first time, many Americans and sectors of the government were coming to realize they must do something to conserve natural resources and the environment. These treasures must be protected from overuse and from destruction by conspicuous consumption. The safety of the environment soon would be at the forefront of the nation's concerns.

Chapter Five

Work

At the start of the 1940s, over 8 million Americans, or 14.6 percent of the labor force, was unemployed. Effects of the Great Depression still lingered, but when the country entered World War II in December 1941, everything dramatically changed.

Shortly after Japan attacked Pearl Harbor, Hawaii, and the United States entered the war, President Franklin Roosevelt set a goal for America's factories. He challenged workers to build 60,000 airplanes, 40,000 tanks, 20,000 anti-aircraft guns, and 8 million tons of merchant ships for carrying supplies. (Ship production is often measured in tons rather than the number of individual ships.) He also asked that all this be done by the end of 1942. In 1943 and 1944, he set even higher goals—and each time American workers met the challenge. By the end of the war, the United States had the world's most powerful economy.

World War II had transformed the workplace. The need for factory workers helped open up new opportunities for minorities and for women in the factories making weapons and supplies for the military. Scientific and technological breakthroughs made during the war led to new kinds of jobs after the war, in fields such as electronics, plastics, and the brand new computer industry. The new television industry also needed workers, from behind-the-scene office workers to on-air stars.

For some workers after the war, new technology also created

Women work on the body of an airplane (LEFT) **during World War II** (National Archives); **secretaries at work in New York City** (RIGHT) **in 1952.** (Library of Congress)

new challenges. Companies found that some of the new technology could help their companies become even more productive. This meant fewer workers were needed. Labor unions that had become very powerful during World War II resisted any changes that would cost laborers their jobs.

Technology also changed America's farms. During the 1940s and 1950s, many farms were purchased by large companies known as "agribusinesses." These farms used the latest in farming techology to produce more crops than ever before. At the same time, however, the number of people working on America's farms fell steadily.

Technology and Automotives

World War II and then competition with the Soviet Union after the war helped open and sponsor new technologies, such as electronics, plastics, and the newly born computer industry. Jobs developing and manufacturing these "high-tech" products rapidly grew in number. For example, people found work in the little-known field of computer programming and development. Others were making practical applications for the work computers could do. Still others were out in the field, selling the latest computers to large businesses, universities, or the military.

Most "high-technology" company employees had learned their basic skills in an institution of higher education. It was the same with sales staff, managers, and administrators. College was becoming a requirement for a good career. By the late 1950s, with so many Americans entering college, there was a severe shortage of skilled plumbers, carpenters, electricians, and mechanics. The nation was undergoing a long-running building boom. New homes were going up in suburbs around the cities, but the tradesmen to build them were hard to find. New housing starts totaled 603,000 in 1940, and rose to almost 1.3 million in 1960. Also, the 1956 Federal Highway Act funded the interstate highway system. That project required thousands more workers in the building trades. Eventually, they built a 42,500-mile network of roads linking America's cities.

The rapid growth of the automotive industry also brought new employment opportunities. Jobs were available in thousands of new auto repair shops and gas stations. The industry itself required thousands of workers for its assembly lines at plants.

High Technology, Low Employment

The computer industry slowly took shape after the pioneering successes of the 1940s. The first computer controlled by software was developed in 1941. This was soon followed by the first electronic digital computer that stored data, and also by magnetic calculating machines. In 1948, Bell Laboratories invented the transistor, a tiny electronic device for controlling the flow of electric current. Only a few computers were built and sold—mostly to institutions such as laboratories and universities. Employment in the field was limited mainly to inventors and technicians.

In 1954, about 200 computers were built. In 1957, the number was more than 1,000, showing a notable increase in computer use. When the Russians launched *Sputnik*, the first manmade satellite, in October 1957, improving computer technology became essential to the space race that followed. More jobs opened up for computer programmers, and for hardware and software developers. In 1959, American engineers invented the "microchip," a miniature electronic circuit especially for computers. This was a major technological breakthrough. The speed and capacity of the microchip revolutionized the computer industry. Developers created ever smaller computers that operated with lightning speed. But the typical computer was still a room-size "mainframe."

As computers were adapted and designed for space and military uses, they also found a place in civilian life. In the 1960s, the exciting world of computers could be seen on the horizon by those who followed its development. New employees were now needed in every aspect of the field. Eventually, a professional sales staff would introduce this new technology to American business. One day, computer manufacturers would sell their products to the average consumer, who as yet knew next to nothing about them.

One of the earliest computers was known as ENIAC, or Electronic Numerical Integrator And Computer. The 150-foot-wide computer was developed during World War II at the University of Pennsylvania. (Library of Congress)

The industry was based mainly in the industrial Midwest, especially in Michigan. Detroit became the center of automobile manufacturing. It employed vast research and design staffs as well as marketing and advertising departments to promote and sell the latest models.

Industry and Unions

American manufacturers dominated world commerce, from automobiles to shipbuilding. By the 1950s, however, there was increasing overseas competition in countries that had recovered from World War II. Progressive manufacturers in Germany, Japan, and Italy were building modern plants with the newest equipment. At the same time, much of American industry was beginning to age. Steel manufacturing, in particular, suffered from old equipment that too often broke down or was not as productive as new equipment. Foreign steelmakers offered cheaper and sometimes better steel than did American mills. Americans lost business.

Much difficulty was caused by labor unions who were unwilling to agree to modernization of plants. The unions—also known as trade unions—feared that modern equipment would cut down the number of workers a plant needed. For this reason, they opposed many advances in manufacturing techniques. Union members often fought to delay modernization. Sometimes they even sabotaged new equipment they did not want to use.

The labor unions were extremely strong through most of the 1940s and 1950s. Their members were better paid than non-union workers. Also, unions protected the jobs of their members by uniting to bargain with employers for better wages and working conditions. The ideal blue-collar job was on the automobile assembly line, where wages were high and the

FDR Ends Workplace Discrimination

Before World War II, African Americans were generally kept out of high-paying jobs in factories and other workplaces. In 1940, A. Philip Randolph, head of Brotherhood of Sleeping Car Porters, the largest all–African American labor union, began to put pressure on President Franklin Roosevelt to change the situation. When Roosevelt resisted, Randolph threatened to bring 100,000 African Americans to Washington, D.C., for a protest march.

In response, President Roosevelt agreed to ban racial discrimination in defense industries. The next year, the Fair Employment Practices Committee for war industries was created by executive order.

unions were powerful. Virtually every auto worker was a United Auto Workers union member. Teachers also developed some of the best-organized unions in the country in these years. They grew in power each time their strikes won better working conditions and higher wages. Like other unions, teachers' organizations could offer thousands of votes to candidates whose policies were in agreement with their own.

Often, when large unions went on a general strike at a number of job locations, the effects were national. Major strikes in the coal industry, for example, could disrupt the entire economy. A shortage of coal caused problems in almost every aspect of life, from manufacturing to construction to home heating. Thus, trade unions had great influence in both the economy and in politics. This influence became even stronger in 1955, when the two largest associations of trade unions merged. The American Federation of Labor and the Congress of Industrial Organizations combined into the new AFL-CIO, with 15 million members.

Many Americans, especially executives and business people, disliked trade unions. They resented unions' political power and willingness to strike. Unions also gained a reputation for corruption. The worst had leaders who cheated in the organization's elections and often were associated with organized crime. Some stole money from their union's treasury or from pension funds set up to help members after retirement.

One of the most notorious was the International Brotherhood of Teamsters. It represented truckers and related workers in the transportation industry. With more than 350,000 members in 1940, the Teamsters' was the nation's largest union. In 1957, this union was accused of corruption and thrown out of the AFL-CIO. It continued to operate and became perhaps the single most powerful labor organization, with more than 1.83 million members.

The movement of business and industry out of the Northeast and Midwest and into the South weakened unions. As northern factory workers lost their jobs, they found their union membership of little use. Local union chapters were forced to close when the employers left. Fewer Americans were joining unions by the end of the 1950s, and unions were losing their political and economic power.

The number of work stoppages involving 1,000 workers or more indicates the growth of union power. It also shows its steady decline. In 1950 there were 424 major work stoppages by approximately 1.7 million workers. In 1960 that figure dropped to 222 stoppages involving 896,000 employees.

Women at Work

In 1940, women in the labor force numbered 12.84 million. They represented about 25 percent of women 16 and older, and 24 percent of the total American labor force. By 1950, 18.4 million women were working, representing almost 34 percent of females of working age. Women were now 29 percent of the total labor force, an increase of five percent over 1940. By 1960, working women numbered more than 23.26 million. This was almost 38 percent of working-age women and more than 32.5 percent of the total labor force.

Before World War II, the government restricted women from working in certain jobs, such as heavy industry. Married women were not supposed to work at all. Because so many men left for the war, the federal government had to officially reclassify jobs so women could take them. The government also made discrimination because of race illegal.

At first, only single women were wanted in the workforce, but there were not enough to fill all the jobs. In 1943, married women were also allowed to work. Many women worked at jobs traditionally held by men—manufacturing, welding, handling riveting guns, working with steel, and building airplanes and military equipment. After the war, when the men returned, most women left these jobs—voluntarily or not. Many became housewives, raising families. A few years after the war, however, women began to go back into the workforce.

Although women often did the same work as white men, they usually were paid less—as were all minority employees. Some women and African Americans objected, but most accepted the situation and the lower pay. As these decades passed, working women earned steadily less than working men earned. In 1947, the median income earned by women was about 45 percent of men's. In 1960, women's median income declined to less than 31 percent of what men earned. By the mid-1950s, many women were beginning to demand equal pay. Not until 1963 did federal law prohibit unequal treatment of women and minorities in the workplace.

Nursing was one of the most highly regarded professions for young women. But the pay was low and the conditions extremely difficult. There were ever-increasing requirements for education and training. The registered nurse (RN) had to study ever harder before earning proper credentials. The RN was the backbone of the medical profession, especially in hospitals. Overworked RNs took on more and more responsibility for the care of patients and even for their diagnosis. As medicine became more complex, additional training for RNs was required. By the end of this era, nursing remained a much-respected profession. But its poor pay, high stress, and long hours made it less desirable than previously.

Many women who wanted a stable, respectable job that offered a sense of satisfaction and pride became school teachers. By the end of the 1950s, strong teachers' unions and a national quest for educational excellence improved the status of teachers, men and women both. Women were increasingly becoming elementary school principals and administrators, positions formerly held by men.

In 1958, jet airline passenger service was established by National Airlines between New York City and Miami. This was the first service within the United States, but it soon expanded. With the increase in air travel, an attractive career was rapidly expanding for ambitious women: the airline stewardess, or flight attendant.

The Professional Office Worker

By the mid-1940s, women were the majority in office staffs. They worked as secretaries, receptionists, and filing clerks. A few decades previous, only white men were private secretaries to leading businessmen. As mid-century was reached, the best secretaries were mainly white women. The profession was more and more considered a top-notch career for a woman. Even though office staff were paid low wages, these jobs at the center of fast-moving business and industry had high social status. Movies and television portrayed well-dressed, glamorous secretaries working closely with their wealthy and handsome male bosses. They often proved to be just as smart and capable.

Employment as a business secretary was extremely desirable. Special schools developed to educate women in business and secretarial skills. While men took their places in factories and on the assembly line, many women aimed to become secretaries. Office workers were so much in demand that the Russell Kelly Office Services opened in 1947. It became a swift success by offering temporary office help. These "temps" became known as Kelly Girls. As American business grew, temps became essential to the operations of thousands of offices.

Some "Kelly Girls" from Russell Kelly Office Services on a promotional bus tour during the late 1950s. The Kelly Girl logo (TOP). (Courtesy of Kelly Office Services)

Another major field opened up to women with business skills in the 1940s and 1950s—government. At every level, from county and state to the federal government, employment grew rapidly. In this time, bigger governments were appearing everywhere around the country. New social programs required bureaucracies to administer them. Local communities and states were improving roads and bridges and offering more and better services to their populations. All this needed management, administrators, staff, clerks, and librarians.

In 1940, 4.47 million Americans were employed by federal, state, and local governments. By 1960, that figure almost doubled to 8.8 million. The federal government, with 2.42 million, employed more than one-fourth of the total in 1960. State governments employed 1.52 million, and another 4.86 million worked for local governments. This public employment benefited both national and local economies. Payrolls from all three levels jumped from $556 million in 1940 to $3.33 billion in 1960.

Pop Stars, Promoters, and Dreamers

American industry and business thrived through the 1950s. Many young people dreamed of a different profession than their parents knew. The rise of television and the growth of the entertainment industry offered employment opportunities. Many television stations were established in the mid-1940s and early 1950s. Although many people wanted to be movie or television stars, there were thousands of other jobs to be filled.

These stations and the new national broadcast networks hired all sorts of employees, from station managers to announcers, office staff to maintenance workers, writers to set designers and sales staff who sold advertising time.

The advertising business influenced the kinds of programs permitted on radio and television. Ever since 1941, when the Bulova Watch company sponsored the first television commercial, advertisers set the standards for what would be broadcast. "It's Bulova Watch Time" was a familiar advertising message seen again and again by Americans watching television. Soft drinks such as Pepsi and Coke, and dozens of automobile manufacturers, would eventually dominate advertising on the airwaves. Creating that advertising was another growing field for talented Americans. Workers could create and write ads or work in the fast-paced business side of advertising agencies.

Hollywood offered the most opportunity for employment in the movie world, while New York City had the television networks and the advertising agencies. Book publishing, too, was centered in New York, where editorial and marketing offices were headquartered. Books were usually printed within fifty miles of Manhattan.

Recorded music exploded in this period. That industry was scattered around the country. Hit songs might come out of Philadelphia, Detroit, Nashville, or Memphis, as well as New York or Los Angeles. Both 45 rpm (singles) and 33 rpm (long-playing, or LP) records came into widespread use in the 1940s. Magnetic recording tape was developed by the end of the decade, but was not much used by the public. The enormous "music business" involved much more than live stage or broadcast performances. Recorded music reached the entire nation and other countries, where American culture was appealing to young people. In 1946, jukeboxes began to be mass-produced. Soon they were found in every restaurant, bar, and soda fountain. Stores selling only records competed with record sections in the new department stores of the suburban malls.

Farming Declines

Bounding American prosperity made Americans the best fed people in the world. This prosperous public assured a ready market for fruit, vegetables, grains, livestock, and dairy products. The United States was also ship-ping millions of tons of food to other nations. Many were still suffering from the destruction of war. Others could not produce food as cheaply as the United States.

Mechanization of farms and the development of huge agricul-tural corporations gave the coun-try an advantage internationally. Corporate farming—agribusi-ness—had the capacity for enor-mous production. It also kept prices low. While agribusiness was profitable, small, family farms failed steadily. They were unable to compete in price or quantity.

Millions of young people on farms rose early to feed stock or help with milking, before going off to school. At the end of the day, they had many more chores—feeding chickens, loading hay, helping repair fences, and usually another round of milking. They had to do all this as well as their homework. The three months of summer vacation was a valued American tradition because most children lived on the farm. By the late 1940s, the majority of American teens, who did not live on farms, found paying summer jobs—working in retail establishments or doing odd jobs like mowing lawns, or babysitting, for instance. More than any generation before, young people who matured in the 1950s earned their own spending cash. They were the youngest and largest "consumer-generation" of all.

Farm children, however, had only a little pocket money. They were not paid anywhere near as well as city and suburban children, who often worked in stores or restaurants. Though they worked extremely hard, long hours, family farmers were almost always in debt and seldom had much ready cash. By the 1950s, their children had other dreams than working on the farm morning till night. Most of those dreams were inspired by watching the "good life" in movies and on television. The farm was loved by the latest generation of farm children, but they wanted an easier life.

An hourly wage, a regular check, and lighter working conditions could be found in the cities. There factories and construc-

Migrant farmworkers, such as these, moved from place to place harvesting carrots (FACING PAGE), **spinach** (LEFT), **cabbage** (RIGHT), **and other crops.** (National Archvies)

tion boomed through the 1950s. Many young people left the farm, never to return. Their aging parents came to realize there would be no one to replace them. Corporate agribusiness took advantage of this situation. It bought up farms from such parents, expanding operations to hundreds of thousands of acres.

There was considerable work to be had in agribusiness. Main areas of employment included plowing fields, planting and cultivating and harvesting crops, and feeding breeding and milking livestock. Employees were needed to maintain equipment and buildings, and to erect and repair fences. In corporate agriculture, many of these jobs required trained employees.

Unskilled farm workers migrated from farm to farm, north to south, east to west, according to the growing season and the availability of work. They were known as migrant farm workers. These employees were paid well below the minimum wage. They had few rights and no union to protect them. Most of them were Mexican American or Mexican citizens who came to the United States to work. Their employment and temporary living conditions were more miserable than any family farmer would accept for themselves. Migrant workers had no ownership in the lands or crops they worked. Yet, the wages were far better than what they could earn in Mexico.

Cheap farm labor combined with mechanization and rapid shipment of crops to market to make America the world's leading food-producing nation. Between 1940 and 1960, cash income from American agriculture grew from $9.1 billion to almost $35 billion. This powerful economic position in the world of food production did little to help family farmers. Nor did it lift Mexican American farm workers out of poverty.

Despite the changes in the workplace and on the farm, work was generally plentiful in the 1950s. Howoever, at the close of the era, the unemployment rate was 6.8 percent of the labor force, the highest it had been since 1940.

Chapter Six

Religion

In the middle of the twentieth century, Americans remained strongly religious. However, how people practiced their faiths changed as some major American faiths lost membership in the 1940s and 1950s, while others gained.

In 1940, ninety-five percent of Americans had been born into a family that was Christian or Jewish. Approximately 87 percent still claimed to belong to a religion. Although only 40 percent actually attended houses of worship regularly, Americans had a firm belief system. They believed in a divine being or power who had responsibility for the world.

Most Americans practiced a religion that was closely tied to the family life of their parents and grandparents. Religion was strongly cultural, linked to old traditions and ways. Some faiths had been brought to America by immigrants during the past seventy-five years. Others had been in the United States since colonial days.

The America of the mid-twentieth century was strongly Christian, especially Protestant. After Christians, Jews were the next largest religious group, at five percent of the population. The rest of Americans either had no religion or were members of small religious groups. These other faiths included Buddhism, Islam, and Native American tribal worship, as well as rites, such as Voodoo, based on African traditions.

Hispanic Americans leave church services (LEFT) in New Mexico; a group of girls singing in their church choir during the mid-1940s (RIGHT). (Library of Congress)

By the end of this era, there was growing interest in religion that until then had been almost invisible. More than ever before, Americans were expressing tolerance—acceptance of faiths that were different from their own. Many people felt a powerful urge toward ecumenism, a coming together of faiths for better understanding and friendship.

Inside and Outside Christianity

Protestantism was the largest religion in the 1940s, counting for 69 percent of the American population. Protestants included many different denominations, or sub-groups, with similar basic beliefs. These included Baptists, Methodists, Episcopalians, Lutherans, Unitarians, Presbyterians, and Dutch Reformed. Many of these groups were further divided by race or disputes over religious teachings. Some Protestant denominations had beliefs held by the majority of colonial Americans. The beliefs of New England's Puritans were handed down to the group called Congregationalist. In 1940, many Presbyterians, Methodists, and Episcopalians still worshiped in churches built during the seventeenth and eighteenth centuries.

Baptists had grown faster than any other Protestant denomination. They were divided into four main groups. There were the evangelical, mostly white Southern Baptists. (Evangelical Christians beleive that it is their duty to actively spread the teachings of Jesus to others.) A second Baptist group was the less evangelical and sometimes racially integrated American Baptists. Two other Baptist groups were largely African American: the National Baptist Convention of America and the National Baptist Convention, U.S.A. In 1940, Baptists accounted for about 35 percent of Protestants aged 16 or older. The Baptist percentage of the Protestant population reached a high of approximately 37 percent in the mid-1950s. In 1940, Methodists were about 24 percent of Protestants. By the mid-1950s they had declined to around 18 percent. Lutherans were the next largest Protestant group, with 12 percent of the total in 1940, down to about 10 percent by the end of the 1950s.

In these decades, the largest single Christian faith was Roman Catholicism, with 20 percent of the total population. Although Catholics were united by common leadership and the Latin language of their services, individual churches often

When these Japanese Americans attended a Buddhist service in 1943, few non-Asian Americans practiced the religion in the United States. In the decades that followed more non-Asian Americans would explore Buddhism and other Eastern religions. (Library of Congress)

formed by ethnic group, such as Irish, Italian, or Mexican American.

In the 1940s and early 1950s, most other American religious traditions were brought by Asians. Largely from Japan and China, these peoples practiced Buddhism, Confucianism, and Shintoism. They lived mainly in the coastal cities of California and the Northeast.

Early in the twentieth century, several thousand Muslim immigrants came from the Middle East. Among them were Syrians, many of whom settled in Iowa. Lebanese-Syrian communities grew up in North Dakota. Other Islamic communities appeared in Michigan, Pennsylvania, and Indiana.

In the 1930s, a group of African Americans adopted a form of the Muslim faith and became known as the Nation of Islam. Later known as Black Muslims, the group promoted pride in African American heritage. Black Muslims were mainly recruited from northern cities, where they established their mosques.

World War II and American Jews

In the decades before the 1940s, anti-Jewish feeling had been close to the surface in the United States. Anti-Semitism (hatred of

Jews) reached a peak in the years between the world wars. Most American Jews had family ties with European Jews. It was frightening to hear of intensifying persecution by the Nazis.

In this time, many colleges, private schools, summer camps, hotels, and employers put limitations on accepting or hiring Jews. There were physical threats to Jews by the Ku Klux Klan. This secret group attacked Jews, Catholics, and racial minorities.

By late 1939, the federal government was aware that Jews were being oppressed in Nazi Europe. Still, it refused to accept a ship carrying more than 900 Jewish refugees who were escaping from Germany. The government did not want to be involved in the controversy. World War II began that year, although the United States did not yet take part.

In 1941, the United States was attacked by Japan and entered the war. This made the communist Soviet Union an American ally against the fascist dictatorships. During the war, many Jews fought bravely in the American military, proving their loyalty.

These women and children were freed when the concentration camp at Lambach, Austria, was overrun by the 71st Infantry Division. Before the United States entered the war, Jewish refugees fleeing Nazi Germany were turned away from the United States. (National Archives)

Then, in the middle of the war, reports of wholesale Nazi massacres of Jews reached America. Widespread sympathy arose for the Jewish people. By 1944, a temporary camp for Jewish war refugees was opened at Oswego, in upstate New York.

Jewish persecution at the hands of the Nazis, a time known as the Holocaust, cost Europe most of its Jewish population. More than six million Jews are estimated to have died. After the war, the United States had the world's largest Jewish population, more than 4.5 million persons. In these years, American Jews worked hard to help establish the state of Israel as the Jewish homeland. Early in 1948, Israel became an independent state, and their dream was realized.

Another symbol of Jewish achievement was the founding of Brandeis University in Massachusetts, also in 1948. Brandeis was the first Jewish-sponsored, nonsectarian (nonreligious), institution of higher education in America. As a group, Jews achieved remarkable educational and business accomplishments in this time. A large number of Jews were successful financially, and they rose in society during the 1950s. Jews were being elected as prominent politicians, serving as key advisers to presidents, and taking a lead in the nation's cultural life.

At the start of the 1940s, Jews lived mostly in New York and Chicago. The Jewish community was spreading out now, finding new homes in cities such as Los Angeles and Miami. This brought Jewish influence to an ever-wider part of American life. Jewish families also moved in large numbers to the suburbs. There, they lived the prosperous middle-class lives that their parents and grandparents had only dreamed of.

Catholics also Overcome Prejudice

At the start of the 1940s, Catholic Americans also faced strong prejudice. Over the centuries, hostility between Protestants and Catholics in Europe often had erupted in long and bloody wars. Resentments from those age-old conflicts still existed in the United States of the 1940s.

Protestants had arrived first in early America. Although Maryland had been founded by Catholics, most Catholics came later, after the middle nineteenth century. For centuries, Protestants kept Catholics out of public office. It was even difficult for Catholics to enter mainstream journalism and banking.

Catholic services at a church in El Cerrito, New Mexico. (National Archives)

One reason for anti-Catholic feelings was that American Protestants feared that the pope and the Catholic Church would acquire too much political power.

Through the first half of the twentieth century, Catholics created dynamic business and cultural worlds of their own. They established parochial schools, and Catholic-run universities, hospitals, and community centers. There were Catholic radio and television shows, magazines, newspapers, and book publishers.

Change Takes Root

In 1950, several mainstream Protestant denominations formed an alliance, in part to strengthen their political standing. The National Council of Churches was a coalition of seven mainstream denominations: American Baptists, Congregationalists, Disciples, Episcopalians, Lutherans, Methodists, and Presbyterians. This new group worked together to create a voting bloc that was the strongest religious force in American politics. For the next ten years, the Protestant establishment continued to dominate the American religious and political scene.

The National Council of Churches also became active in ecumenical and interfaith activities. It took the lead in promoting understanding among all religions. It also countered the more conservative fundamentalist Protestant trends that had developed in the 1920s and 1930s in opposition to Darwin's theory of evolution.

By the end of the 1950s, other faiths were making their mark as they grew in membership and strength. These included the Jehovah's Witnesses, Seventh-Day Adventists, Christian Scientists, and Latter Day Saints (or Mormons). The Mormons, based in Salt Lake City, Utah, would eventually become one of the fastest-growing religions, mainly in the far West.

The Civil Rights movement of this era was led by religious organizations. By the 1950s, the growing quest for civil rights rose out of various black churches. The inspiration for public action came largely from African American denominations of the Baptist Church. So did much of the movement's leadership. Alabama preacher, Martin Luther King, Jr., was the greatest leader of the Civil Rights movement. King was supported by a broad coalition known as the Southern Christian Leadership Conference. Many Protestant and Catholic Christians and Jews actively supported the Civil Rights movement. Nonviolence and high moral and religious righteousness were at the heart of the movement and key to its eventual triumph. Civil rights cooperation helped change, for the better, how religions thought about one another.

As the 1950s came to a close, change was also facing the Catholic Church. Many Catholics openly questioned church doctrine and papal authority. Some wanted greater participation by members in the mass. (The mass is a series of prayers and ceremonies that honor the sacrifice of Jesus Christ.) Others wanted more decision-making authority for their own parishes and less control from Rome. Many asked to hear the mass said in English, not in Latin, as it always had been. At the same time, a shortage of priests began to develop as fewer men entered the priesthood.

In 1959, Pope John XXIII called for a gathering of bishops and church leaders to discuss the future of the church. Named the Second Vatican Council, its purpose was to renew the spirituality and attitudes of the church. Also, the Catholic Church wanted to join with other Christian religions in a search for new understanding and cooperation.

The Kennedy Presidency

By the mid-1950s, many Americans had become more accepting of people of different religions. This more-accepting attitude was indicated by a survey that asked whether Americans would vote for a "well-qualified" Jew or Catholic for president. In 1940, about 45 percent said they would vote for a Jewish presidential candidate, and 55 percent said they would vote for a Catholic. By 1960, about 72 percent said they would vote for a Jew, and 74 percent for a Catholic.

At the same time, objections to marriage between people of different religions were also falling away. In 1940, 13 percent of American couples were of different religions. By 1960, that figure was above 20 percent.

Also helping to merge cultures were the many great Jewish and Catholic stars in sports, music, film, literature, and on the stage. Perhaps the most prominent Catholic of the era was John F. Kennedy, elected president in 1960. Kennedy was the first Catholic ever to hold that office. As president, Kennedy disproved the notion that a Catholic president would put loyalty to the Pope above loyalty to the nation.

The grandson of a poor Irish immigrant who had come to America and made a fortune, Kennedy became one of the best-loved presidents of all. Americans of every faith believed Kennedy's presidency opened a new era of positive change and optimism.

Pluralism and Diversity

Through the 1950s, the Protestant, Catholic, and Jewish faiths remained the most widely practiced faiths in the United States. By the end of the decade, however, some in the baby boom generation were losing interest in these religions. While some stopped participating in organized religion altogether, other faiths began to attract new followers. They also began to explore different faiths, including Buddhism and other Eastern religions.

A search for new religious meaning was developing in the younger generation. Many wanted to find common ground among the various beliefs. This trend joined a worldwide move toward ecumenism. People of different faiths examined one another's customs and beliefs.

Religion and Community

People came to houses of worship for more than just religious services. In small towns and large cities, family and community events such as dances, lectures, bake sales, and weddings were regularly held in houses of worship. They could be in city cathedrals or suburban synagogues, country churches or storefront meeting halls. Here, there was space for community meetings. Scouting troops, garden clubs, arts and craft groups, and civic-improvement organizations were welcome. Many prosperous houses of worship had gymnasiums for recreation, with basketball courts and leagues for youth and adult play.

Much of America's sense of community and belonging was found in local churches and synagogues. On national holidays, congregations united to celebrate, to march in parades, and show their patriotism. At times of crisis, houses of worship were centers for gathering to offer mutual support. If a family suffered a loss, perhaps a death or a fire, the congregation was there to help. Religion was dynamic and essential to Americans in the 1940s and 1950s.

Yet, it was also changing in many ways. Television and movies were introducing new ideas, new values. By the end of the 1950s, new social movements challenged the prejudices that once had kept religions hostile to one another.

By 1960, a time of great change in religion was in store. One of the most powerful characteristics of America's religious life in the coming era would be its diversity.

Chapter Seven

Health, Science, and Technology

A public health poster (LEFT) **issued during World War II. An electrical power generating station** (RIGHT). **During the 1940s and 1950s, electrical power reached most homes in the United States for the first time.** (National Archives)

The Electric Age is probably the most appropriate description for the mid-twentieth century. Even the so-called Atomic Age, or the Space Age, was not as important as the electrification of America. Atomic power and space technology would never have come to be without electricity. Bringing electricity to the nation was one of the great successes of the 1940s and 1950s.

Electricity made all else possible, from medical research that conquered polio to satellites that shot into orbit around the planet. Radio and television also depended on electricity, both to broadcast programs and to make the equipment that received them. By the late 1950s, life without electricity was unthinkable. Most new and indispensable products, from automobiles to cameras, were made using electrical power. These products also contained the world's newest wonder material: plastic. The combination of electricity and plastics would make all other technological developments possible from now on.

At first, atomic power seemed to be the answer to the fast-growing need for electricity. Yet there were questions about the use of nuclear technology. Was it really safe for human beings? Doubts remained in the background as American progress in every possible field roared onward through the 1950s.

Electrifying America

Electricity was the single most important factor in modernizing twentieth-century American life. Before 1940, the power industry developed rapidly. New generating plants were built, and transmission lines went up. Millions of older homes, farms, and businesses were "wired," one by one, for electricity. Private power companies constructed most of the generating plants and erected power lines into populated areas. When it came to lightly populated rural regions, however, utilities considered them unprofitable to electrify. In the years before World War II, only 10 percent of American farms had electricity.

By the 1940s, state and federal agencies were taking charge of electrifying rural regions. In 1945, almost half of all farms had been electrified. This dramatically improved both agricultural production and the farm family's daily life. Government agencies, such as the Tennessee Valley Authority and the Rural Electrification Administration, worked hard to electrify the nation. They saw to it that almost every community in the United States was electrified by the end of the 1950s. Major new systems of dams generated hydroelectric power—electricity created by water flow running a generator. Other power plants burned coal or oil to run their generators.

The government agencies that oversaw electrification proved the private companies wrong. It was indeed profitable to electrify the countryside and the poorer communities. The need for electricity grew faster than new systems could be built. After World War II, there was great public demand for electrical appliances and equipment. From 1947 on, electrical usage increased an average of 8 percent a year. Every ten years, the amount of electricity used was twice that of ten years earlier.

With technological improvements in generating equipment and transmission lines, electricity became ever cheaper to produce and distribute. The rising demand for power stimulated construction of more power plants, increasing electrical output. Improvements in productivity brought the price of electricity down. In 1900, electricity had been a luxury item that, in 1992 dollars, cost $4 a kilowatt hour. By 1947, electricity cost nineteen cents per kilowatt hour in 1992 dollars. The per-kilowatt price kept falling until it was around ten cents by the early 1960s.

Lower production costs encouraged more electricity usage in

business and the home. In the 1940s and 1950s, the power industry strongly promoted the use of electricity. Their advertising slogan was "Live Better Electrically." The idea of an "All-Electric Home" appealed to Americans, who were eager to use electricity in almost every aspect of their lives. The electrification of the United States encouraged families to buy radios and televisions by the millions.

Communications and Broadcasting

At the opening of the 1940s, radio was the family's main source of recorded and live music. Radio stations produced local shows and had their own announcers. They aired musicians who performed in their studios and they also played the latest records. Most radio stations operated on the frequency, or "band," known as AM. There was another band called FM, which was little-used. The first FM radio station was W47NV, Nashville, founded in 1941. Stations belonged to national "networks" that provided programming which was broadcast nationwide. These programs included music, comedy, drama, news, and sports.

The invention of the transistor in 1948 was a breakthrough in broadcast technology. A transistor is a tiny electronic device that controls the flow of electric current. It was essential in radio development and for the advancement of telecommunications, which included broadcast media and telephones. Later, the transistor became crucial to the development of computers.

In 1941, the federal government awarded the first commercial television license. It was given to W2XBS, New York City. The postwar growth of television was a severe blow to the radio industry. Radio soon lost much of its advertising revenue to the new broadcast medium. Television swept over the nation like a tidal wave. More than 5,000 households had one by 1946, and 17 million households had televisions by 1951. In this year, the first live coast-to-coast television program was broadcast. This was made possible thanks to improvements in transmission cable and in receiving and amplifying equipment. In 1954, television advertising revenues passed radio for the first time. By then, color television had arrived, stimulating even more interest in TV.

Among the important communications firsts was the development of magnetic recording tape in 1942. Home tape recorders were on the market by 1947. In 1948, home entertainment was advanced with the first long-playing (LP) record. LPs had several tunes on each side, while previous records usually had only one tune to a side. In 1958, recorded music advanced in quality with the first stereo LP records. Record player technology kept up with the recording industry's innovations. The term *high fidelity* became a popular label for the latest record player.

By 1952, broadcast programming could go anywhere now that the pocket-sized transistor radio was on the market. Transistor radios were an enormous success, especially with young people. These radios were inexpensive and easy to carry. Nobody needed to miss a World Series game if they owned a transistor radio.

In 1946, the first mobile, or wireless, telephone was developed. The mobile phone would not come into general public use for several decades. In 1956 the first transatlantic telephone cable was completed, stretching under the ocean from Scotland to Newfoundland. Intercontinental phone calls were possible now, although the sound quality remained dubious for years to come.

During the late 1950s, Bell Laboratories developed this "drive-in" telephone, allowing users to talk on the telephone from their cars for the first time. (Library of Congress)

Television's Impact on Politics

The content of television programming soon changed from all-entertainment to coverage of important national events. Broadcasts included sensational congressional hearings on organized crime in 1951. A vast home audience watched the proceedings. They saw notorious underworld figures and crooked politicians being questioned sharply. Senator Estes Kefauver of Tennessee was head of the investigating commission. Americans were riveted to the screen as Kefauver matched wits with slick, big-city crime figures. As a result of the hearings, he became one of the most famous personalities in the country. This showed the power of television to reach most of the population.

Another major televised event was the 1952 presidential election. A national audience was caught up in the suspense of the Republican convention in Chicago. The cameras of the three major networks revealed the drama up close. With newsmen such as Walter Cronkite of CBS describing it, television showed foot-stamping, sign-waving, chanting delegates. Politicians, bosses, and candidates took center stage for an unprecedented audience of 70 million people. Dwight D. Eisenhower and Richard Nixon became candidates for president and vice president, respectively. They and their wives celebrated enthusiastically on America's television screens.

The next great milestone of national influence for a television broadcast was the Army-McCarthy hearings in 1954. The "star" was Senator Joseph McCarthy of Wisconsin. McCarthy was leading a congressional subcommittee investigation into alleged communist conspiracies. A Republican, he had constructed a vicious "smear" campaign that destroyed the careers of a number of prominent Americans. His victories often were based on lies and bullying, but his influence made him a national figure. Then McCarthy accused the U.S. Army of having communists hidden in its ranks. Army generals stood up to him.

More than 20 million Americans followed the Army-McCarthy hearings. In the end, the entire nation saw McCarthy's true character unmasked. The army and its attorneys came across as honest, courageous victims of McCarthy's slander. In turn, his cruelty and ruthlessness filled the television screen and disgusted viewers. McCarthy's career was immediately destroyed. Congress censured him for going too far with his accusations. Television proved it could present the raw drama of important events. It was a powerful medium that had won the attention of the nation.

In 1960, the first televised presidential political debate climaxed two decades of broadcasting progress. Senator John F. Kennedy faced off with Vice President Nixon before a fascinated national television audience. The underdog, Kennedy, was far more attractive on the screen than the vice president. Kennedy's charm and good looks combined with his eloquence to give him the edge in the debates. Television was key to his narrowly winning the election later that year.

Health and Medicine

By the mid-1950s, it was apparent that Americans were not getting enough exercise. Television kept people inside, and automobiles made it unnecessary to walk. Lack of exercise combined with processed foods, high in sugar and carbohydrates, to make Americans notably less healthy. Heart conditions and diabetes were on the increase, and there was a steady rise in obesity.

Throughout the 1950s, there was little general concern for healthy diets, but a few "health food" stores still appeared. These stores were small and eccentric. They usually specialized in vitamins, food supplements, and various alternative treatments and medicines. Health-food stores had sugar-free "diet food" and juices. These were an alternative to the supermarket's processed foods and the pharmacy's mass-produced drugs. In time, health-food stores would become extremely popular. They would also carry healthy breads, herbal products, and gourmet foods. For most of this era, however, they were seen as being for "health nuts."

Medical developments in these decades were led by the development of antibiotics. The first, streptomycin, an alternative to penicillin, appeared in 1943. Streptomycin was especially effective in treating tuberculosis, a respiratory disease that had been the scourge of the previous hundred years. This antibiotic also proved effective in treating typhoid fever, spinal meningitis, and pneumonia.

Other important medical technology of the period included the use of X-rays for examining a patient's internal condition. There were also a number of important firsts in medicine. In 1943, the Pap smear began to be used for the detection of cervical cancer in women. The first kidney transplant was in 1950, and the first plastic heart valve was installed in 1951. Both procedures would require years before they became routine, however. Heart-valve replacement depended on fast-improving plastics technology that produced materials for replacement parts.

The defeat of polio was one of the great medical achievements of the era. In 1952, a major polio epidemic struck the United States, with more than 50,000 victims. A vaccine developed by Dr. Jonas Salk was tested in this year. Children received the first vaccinations for polio in 1954, and an oral polio vaccine was used

Dr. Jonas Salk (National Archives)

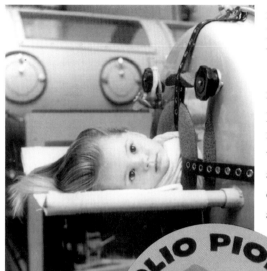

Because polio can paralyze the muscles used to breathe, many polio patients spent their entire lives in iron lungs, devices that forced air in and out of their chests. This little girl (ABOVE), **Regina Edwards, was** photographed at age two during the summer of 1952. In 1954, when the polio vaccine became available, those receiving the first shots to protect against the virus received these "Polio Pioneer" pins (RIGHT) from the National Foundation for Infantile Paralysis. (Library of Congress)

in 1956. Regular improvements in vaccines led to the near-elimination of polio in the United States within the next ten years.

The health of the nation was compromised in 1948 with the invention of the potent pesticide DDT. This poison promised new success in insect control. DDT was extremely effective in killing insects and their larvae. Unfortunately, it was also deadly to birds and other creatures that ate insects. So much DDT was used in these decades that it built up in the soil and entered the ground water. This buildup, and the use of DDT on vegetables and fruits, brought it into the human system. Millions of people suffered from ingesting DDT, but the pesticide's lethal potential was as yet little understood.

The Danger of Smoking

Cigarette smoking became a leading health problem for Americans in the 1940s. Consumption of cigarettes rose rapidly during the war, especially among servicemen and women. Cigarettes were included in the food packages issued to the military. The tobacco companies donated millions of free cigarettes, which was a profitable move. The result was millions of new, addicted smokers.

Cigarette consumption in the United States was 2,558 per capita in 1940. This was nearly twice that of 1930. Smoking would continue to increase. Large-scale advertising was crucial to stimulating smoking. In New York's Times Square, Camel cigarettes' smoke-ring billboard became a landmark in 1941. It would remain there for the next 25 years. Although medical research began to reveal the health dangers of smoking, the tobacco companies flatly denied it. In fact, an important part of their advertising and promotion was to quote doctors touting the benefits of cigarettes. In 1944, Camel ran a full-page ad featuring an army doctor. Part of the text read: "And doctor that he is ... he well knows the comfort and cheer there is in a few moments' relaxation with a good cigarette."

The tobacco industry had powerful financial influence on the media. Tobacco companies sponsored television and radio programs. They advertised heavily in newspapers and magazines. The American media depended on cigarette money for much of their income. Tobacco companies, in turn, depended on modern broadcast and publishing technology to get their message out to the entire population. Because of the tobacco industry's influence, most newspapers and broadcast media did not report on medical findings that linked heart disease and lung cancer to smoking. In fact, many articles appeared that were favorable to smoking. "Why we smoke—We like it," was a feature in a *New York Times* Sunday magazine in 1947.

In 1949, between 44 and 47 percent of all adult Americans smoked; more than 50 percent of men and about 33 percent of women smoked. Studies released in 1948 indicated that lung cancer had grown five times faster than other cancer since 1938. Then, in 1950, three major scientific studies linked smoking to cancer. Although mainstream media still did not publicize the dangers of smoking, many Americans were worried. Tests and reports directly linking smoking and various illnesses were coming out regularly now. Evidence of tobacco's addictive properties also were presented. Cigarette companies still denied any link between smoking and cancer or any other illness. By 1956, lung cancer deaths among white males alone numbered 29,000, compared to 7,000 total lung cancer cases in 1940.

In 1957, the U.S. Surgeon General, the government's top physician, declared cigarette smoking to be a "causative factor" in lung cancer. This was the first time the public health service had taken a position on smoking. That same year, a startling study indicated that babies of mothers who smoked were more often born early and had lower birth weights. Also, they were more likely to be stillborn or die within one month of birth.

By the start of the 1960s, however, smoking was still going strong. There were 70 million smokers in the United States, and tobacco was an $8 billion annual industry. Per-capita consumption of cigarettes had gone up to twelve per day among adults. This was an increase from ten per day in the early 1950s.

Nuclear Science and Its Applications

In World War II, atomic science moved from theory to practical application. The Allies' top-secret Manhattan Project produced an atomic bomb by experimenting with splitting the atom. The first controlled nuclear chain-reaction was in 1942. The next event was the first "A-bomb" test explosion, in 1945, at Alamogordo, New Mexico. Observed by scientists, military leaders, and politicians, this test opened the Atomic Age.

The two atomic bombs dropped on Japan later in 1945 changed warfare forever. The United States now possessed devastating nuclear might. The Soviet Union developed its own atomic bomb a few years later. This brought about the "arms race," a contest to build the world's largest nuclear arsenal. The shadow of nuclear annihilation fell over the world. There was hope that war would be impossible in the future, because its destruction was too terrible.

Testing went on to further improve the power of nuclear bombs. This was often done in secret, underground explosions. An even more destructive hydrogen bomb was developed in the early 1950s. This thermonuclear bomb combined hydrogen with the heat from an exploding atomic bomb to produce the ultimate blast. Experimentation continued until there was a neutron bomb that could kill people but left buildings intact.

Nuclear energy could do more than destroy, however. It could also run electric-generating equipment. This led to nuclear-powered generating plants and ships. In 1954, the first atomic-powered submarine, the USS *Nautilus*, was launched. Two years later, the USS *Polaris* became the first atomic-powered submarine to carry a nuclear warhead. Nuclear submarines did not require fuel oil to operate, which meant they could stay under water much longer than conventional subs. The USS *Enterprise*, the first atomic-powered aircraft carrier, was launched in 1957.

Not all atomic-power applications were for warfare. In 1951, the first American nuclear power plant was built to generate electricity. Atomic-fired power plants seemed to be the perfect method of clean-power generation. They did not pollute the air, as did power plants fired by coal or oil. They did not require vast quantities of fuel that had to be shipped in by endless streams of railroad cars. The material required daily for the nuclear reaction that fired the plant weighed only a few pounds.

The USS *Nautilus*
(National Archives)

The danger of disposing of a power plant's radioactive nuclear waste was still not clear, however. Also, nuclear plants required millions of gallons of water a day to cool their equipment. The resulting warm water that flowed back into the river was deadly for fish populations. Such problems with nuclear power plants were ignored in the 1950s. New plants were regularly built and put into operation around the country.

Flight and the Space Program

Technological improvements in airplanes in the 1940s and 1950s opened vast possibilities in both military and civil aviation. The jet fighters that appeared at the end of World War II became the premier combat aircraft of the Korean War. The first international passenger jet flight was in 1950. At the close of the decade, regular transatlantic jet passenger service was operating from New York to London. In 1958, the first domestic jet airline passenger service began. It was operated by National Airlines and flew between New York City and Miami.

Improvements to jet aircraft required a breed of daring test pilots. They risked their lives flying prototype planes. In 1947, test pilot Chuck Yeager attempted to break the sound barrier for the first time. This meant flying faster than the speed of sound. Yeager risked losing control of his rocket-powered aircraft in his

Chuck E. Yeager, the Air Force pilot who was the first man to fly faster than the speed of sound, sits in the cockpit of the Bell X-1 supersonic research aircraft.
(National Archives)

quest to fly at "supersonic" speed. He would crash if the forces buffeting the aircraft made it too unstable. No one knew what would happen when he flew untested aircraft. Incredibly, Yeager succeeded, breaking the sound barrier and returning to earth safely. He was typical of all courageous test pilots, many of whom died in their duty. Others went on to become the first astronauts. The first woman test pilot, Alma Heflin, flew in 1941.

Supersonic airplanes were in production by the end of the 1940s. They were designed mainly for the military. The first supersonic bomber flew in 1954. Eventually airliners carrying passengers would be capable of flying beyond the sound barrier. The speed and power of rockets and jets were key to the development of the fledgling space program. Building on World War II technical developments, the United States successfully tested its first ballistic missile in 1947. Missiles steadily improved in distance and accuracy. They could be fitted with atomic warheads capable of destroying a city.

Military developments in missile warfare brought about improvements to aircraft design and eventually to spacecraft. These improvements included high-powered fuel and the use of strong, flexible plastics and lighter-weight metals. A new world of control equipment for aircraft and rocketry also emerged. These instruments would rely on computer technology, which was rapidly improving.

In the 1950s, the United States and the Soviet Union both tried to put a man-made satellite into orbit. The Soviets shocked

America in 1957 by launching *Sputnik*, the first earth-orbiting satellite. They had taken the lead in what became known as the space race. *Sputnik* officially opened the Space Age. It was not until the following year that the first American satellite, *Explorer I*, was launched.

The American space program speeded up in 1959 as Congress made additional funding available for research and development. The space race stimulated research into aeronautics and computer technology. Both fields were given major pushes in the hope that the United States would become the leader in space science. In 1959, the USSR stayed ahead of the United States, however, landing the first spacecraft on the moon, *Lunik II*.

The Fruits of Technology

In these decades, many major new concepts were under development. Scientists and inventors worked on new theories, devices, and products. Then skilled technicians figured out how these creations could be used in a practical way. For example, computers, photocopiers, and microwaves had military uses. Later, their technologies were incorporated into home appliances and equipment for the office and industry. First invented in 1947, for example, microwave ovens required more than ten years to be designed for safe installation in kitchens. Many future applications were yet to be devised for the first solar-powered battery when it was invented in 1954.

A number of innovative new products immediately sold well. These included the electric blanket, invented in 1946, and the Polaroid camera, introduced in 1947, which produced almost instant photos. Home chores were made lighter by new products, especially in processed foods. The first prepared cake mixes were on the shelves by 1949, and frozen "TV dinners" were marketed in 1954. Other significant developments included transistorized hearing aids in 1953 and the electric portable typewriter in 1957.

Although it did not directly affect everyday life, the first off-shore oil-drilling platform went into service in 1954. Vast new oil fields in the Gulf of Mexico and off the California coast now could be tapped. In the next decades, oil-drilling platforms appeared by the thousands, working underwater oil fields all around the world.

Edwin Land demonstrates the Polaroid Land camera.
(National Archives)

In 1955, oral contraceptives were developed, freeing women from unwanted pregnancies. At least one new contraceptive proved a disaster, because it caused birth defects in babies. Yet oral contraceptives were part of a new urge toward liberation of women from traditional child-bearing roles.

Automobile technology went forward rapidly. "America's favorite industry," according to auto-company advertising, developed lighter, faster cars. In 1940, synthetic rubber tires appeared. Now it was no longer necessary to tap rubber trees in far-off Asia in order to make tires. Tire technology further improved as the first tubeless tires appeared in 1947. Radial tires went on the market in 1948, offering better handling, safety, and stability. Engine technology also advanced. The first fuel-injection engine came out in 1954, and the Wankel rotary engine arrived in 1957. These engine-design breakthroughs would become widely used in decades to come.

One of the most notable technological feats of the 1950s was the construction of thousands of miles of superhighways. Government funding of construction made money available for the redesign of powerful earthmoving and paving equipment. With these new highways, the American driver had unmatched possibilities for travel and commuting. As a result, auto sales boomed across the nation. Auto-industry prosperity, in turn, stimulated development in the many enterprises, from tires to steel, that were related to automobiles.

In the 1950s, the United States' great wealth made all this technological progress possible. Progress, in turn, made the nation richer, both in material wealth and in the quality of its people's daily lives.

Endless Innovation

After World War II, everything seemed feasible in scientific, health, and technological progress. There was no end to new ideas and products—and plenty of money to pay for them.

Americans had the world's best housing, appliances, goods, and roads. They also shared high expectations that future progress would keep the nation the most modern in the world.

In 1959, there came a major step for science as well as for world peace. The United States, the Soviet Union, and ten other nations signed a pact reserving the continent of Antarctica for peaceful, scientific purposes, never to be militarized.

The World of Plastics

Of all the materials used in manufacturing, goods, and technology, plastics became the most important in this era. After the 1940s, plastics came into ever-wider use, touching everyone's life. By the end of the 1950s, plastics had some involvement with almost every product imaginable. Whether in packaging, manufacturing, or in the products themselves, plastic was everywhere. The decades after 1950 also could be termed the Plastics Age, because so much plastic material was being used.

Plastics are man-made materials. They can be formed into almost any shape and size and include polyethylene, nylon, acrylic, and polyvinyl chloride. The early use of plastics was in billiard balls and coatings for electric cables. By World War II, plastic was being used in military equipment. Airplanes used plastic in place of some metals, which were heavier. Tough and lightweight, polyethylene was used in onboard radar equipment, which until then had been too heavy for aircraft. Radar gave Allied warplanes an advantage in detecting enemy planes first.

After the war, the use and popularity of plastic grew. Polyethylene became the most-used plastic in the world. It was used in soda bottles, milk jugs, and grocery bags. Plastic was used in toys and also as a toy itself. In 1949, a bouncy, plastic putty became one of the most popular toys of all time. First called "Nutty Putty," this plastic could be rolled into a ball that bounced much higher than a rubber ball. It could hold many shapes and be stretched without tearing. It also copied the image from a printed page when pressed against it. More than $6 million worth of "Silly Putty," as it became known, was sold in its very first year.

Throughout the 1940s and 1950s, plastics were crucial to space technology, medical devices, and automobile manufacturing. They were used for textiles, furniture, and computers. In the 1950s, spandex fabric was developed, offering clothing that was flexible yet close-fitting. To replace zippers, velcro was invented around the same time. Its plastic fibers cling to each other to keep things closed or attached.

Plastics were originally developed by scientists searching for material to replace natural products, such as wood and stone. By the end of the 1950s, plastics were the world's most-used material of all.

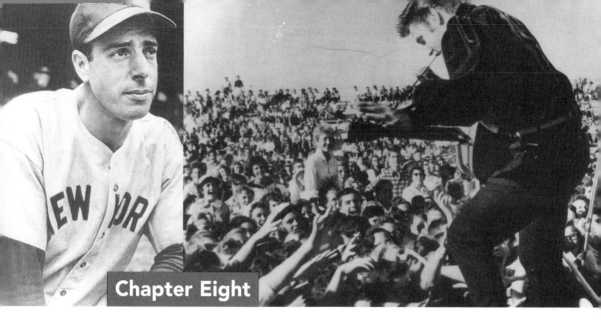

Chapter Eight

Leisure, Sports, and Entertainment

Until the end of World War II, the movies and radio were America's main entertainment media. Americans went regularly to the movies, where they saw dramas and comedies, always accompanied by cartoons. Radio provided most music, variety shows, and dramas.

After the war, television was poised to make its mark. Watching television became the leading family entertainment by the early 1950s. Attendance at the movies dropped dramatically as people stayed home to look at television. Radio, too, had difficulty competing with television.

On Broadway, musicals and serious dramas competed for popular attention. Songs from Broadway shows, recorded by a variety of singers, became top hits.

Music itself underwent a great transition between 1940 and 1960. In jazz, swing gave way to bebop. In pop music, ballads gave way to rock and roll. But Americans listened to a wide variety of music, from jazz to folk songs to classical music.

Playing and watching sports was increasingly part of American daily life. Professional baseball held the nation's attention. It was far more popular than professional football or basketball. Those sports were more popular at the college level. Throughout the era, boxing—both amateur and professional—was popular all over the nation.

Suburban development from 1945 to 1960 spurred participation in several sports. New communities and schools created thousands of public tennis courts and playing fields. Golf courses were built to accommodate the new middle class, which had more leisure time and money to spend. Every suburban area had its bowling alleys, and bowling became a popular leisure activity.

Disneyland seemed to appear magically in Southern California's suburbs in 1955. This amusement park was a perfect complement to Walt Disney's entertainment offerings in film and television. It also symbolized the family's new financial ability to travel for vacations and entertainment.

Television Overtakes Radio

Much early television programming was created by transferring successful shows and stars from radio. Many former radio programs and their stars were extremely successful on television. Comedians Milton Berle, Jack Benny, and the team of George Burns and Gracie Allen brought their variety-show stage acts to TV. They had learned the business in front of live theater audiences. Now they performed in front of a camera—often with live audiences in the television studios. One-liner humor was worked into situation comedies for half-hour shows that captivated America—and soon much of Western Europe, too, as television arrived there.

One of the top situation comedy performers on television was Lucille Ball. A former model for cigarette advertisements, Ball starred in a successful radio program called *My Favorite Husband*. The show, which began in 1947, was about the life of a scatterbrained housewife who was constantly in trouble. In 1951, television executives approached Ball about starring in a television version of her show. She agreed

Lucille Ball and Desi Arnaz (Library of Congress)

to do it on the condition that her husband, Cuban musician Desi Arnaz, play the role of her husband on television. When the executives refused, saying that the American public would never accept an interracial marriage on television, Ball and Arnaz formed their own television studio and produced the show themselves. *I Love Lucy* went on to become one of televisions all-time most beloved programs. Originally running from 1951 to 1957, the show continues in re-runs into the twenty-first century.

Television also gave new life to the careers of fading movie stars. Their films could be seen again by a huge television audience. Comedians Laurel and Hardy, the Marx Brothers, the Three Stooges, and Abbott and Costello became more famous than ever. Reclusive actress Greta Garbo was discovered by an audience that had been too young for her films of the 1920s and 1930s. Even silent films were shown on television. The Keystone Kops and Charlie Chaplin were household words long after their work had been first produced.

Game shows, talk shows, comedies, and variety shows were the nightly television fare of the 1950s. Favorites included *The Ed Sullivan Show*, a variety program seen every Sunday night. Sullivan's programs had everything from popular singers to performing dogs, stand-up comedians to trapeze artists. The show was "family oriented" and wholesome, but Sullivan was a master showman who presented the latest acts. In 1956, he put newcomer Elvis Presley on the air but refused to allow the camera to show the singer's gyrating hips, for fear that his style of dancing would shock the public.

Game shows and quiz shows included *What's My Line?*, a panel of witty celebrities trying to discover a guest's profession. *The $64,000 Question* pitted brainy contestants against each other in a test of stored-up knowledge. *Name That Tune* combined knowledge of popular music with the ability to sprint to the buzzer first. Often contestants started performance careers after singing solo on this show.

A staple of American television was the Western. Cowboy dramas endured through the 1950s and after. Each night of the week, steel-nerved heroes showed off their quick draws and good looks.

Lives of the Stars

Most great performers of the 1940s continued to be popular through the 1950s. These included singers Judy Garland and Mary Martin; former child actor Mickey Rooney; dancers Fred Astaire, Gene Kelly, and Ginger Rodgers; and comedian Danny Kaye. Longtime favorites Katharine Hepburn and Bette Davis were still leading ladies throughout the 1950s. Television broadcasts of old movies gave all their careers new life. They were often the guest performers on television variety shows as well.

In the 1940s and 1950s, crooner Bing Crosby and his comedian partner, Bob Hope, acted together in a series of popular movies such as *The Road to Morocco*. Other heroes of the silver screen, as the movies are sometimes called, included Gary Cooper, Spencer Tracy, Clark Gable, and Errol Flynn. They were joined by rising star Marlon Brando, whose moody characters were far different from the good-natured leading men of the past.

Bing Crosby
(Library of Congress)

Female dramatic leads changed style in the late 1940s. The dark, dignified aura of Garbo and Ingrid Bergman gave way to the blonde. The new stars were led by Marilyn Monroe, the "blonde bombshell," who first appeared in the early 1950s. Besides her sexy looks, Monroe was a gifted actress who played comedy as well as drama. Other blondes, including Grace Kelly, Kim Novak, and Debbie Reynolds, appealed to middle America in these years. Young women who were not so pert or blonde could identify with the Italian Sophia Loren and the American Natalie Wood, who were both glamorous and believable.

Stars like Elizabeth Taylor and Grace Kelly were followed as much for the intrigue and romance of their private lives as for their performances. As a teenager in the mid-1940s, Taylor appeared in the hit movie *National Velvet*. Photographers and gossip

Marilyn Monroe (LEFT);
Elizabeth Taylor (RIGHT)
(Library of Congress)

Life, a Magazine

In the 1940s, the favorite family periodical was the *Saturday Evening Post*. The magazine's humorous covers by illustrators such as Norman Rockwell reflected American home life.

By contrast, *Life* magazine's hard-hitting news features combined punchy writing with dramatic photographs. In the 1950s, it caught up with the *Post*. Television cameramen were not yet as agile as *Life*'s photojournalists, who could move quickly to produce the human-interest photo essay. These features ranged from a day in the life of a beleaguered country doctor to a Harlem gang leader's dangerous existence.

Appearing on the cover of *Life* guaranteed a major boost to the careers of film stars, authors, and politicians. Long before he became president, John F. Kennedy was often pictured in *Life*. Before World War II, he and his family had appeared with his father, the U.S. ambassador to Britain. JFK again appeared in *Life* as the handsome young candidate for the U.S. Senate in 1952. The following year, the magazine featured the wedding of Kennedy and Jacqueline Bouvier. It was "just like a coronation," the editors said. Thanks to *Life*, the Kennedys were national celebrities. The magazine recorded the birth of their daughter, Caroline, then his election as president.

Life was still going strong, but had fierce competition from *Look* magazine. These large-format weekly magazines suffered as television improved. By 1960, the *Post* was failing, soon to close down.

reporters closely followed her film career and many marriages. In 1950, the whole country read about the wedding of 18-year-old Taylor to hotel magnate Conrad Hilton in Beverly Hills. In years to come, Taylor's many divorces and weddings would be news. Kelly often played "the girl next door" on screen. When she married Prince Ranier of Monaco in 1956, she became Princess Grace, whose life seemed a fairy tale to her admirers.

Cartoons and Fantasyland

Few stars of the silver screen were more popular than Bugs Bunny. A cartoon figure created by Warner Brothers for their "Looney Tunes" series, Bugs was a wise guy with a Brooklyn accent. He was forever pitted against the scheming hunter Elmer Fudd, or he matched wits with the jealous Daffy Duck. Cartoon characters were regulars in movie houses. Cartoons were always the openers before the show and often between double features. In the 1950s, television showed old and new cartoons for hours a day. Dozens of cartoon characters, from Porky Pig to Tweety Bird, became well-known.

Family recreation took a spectacular turn in 1955, when Disneyland was built in Anaheim, California. Disneyland gave new meaning to the popular amusement park, and famous Disney characters from film and television came to life. Mickey Mouse, Snow White, and Sleeping Beauty all were there on Disneyland's 160 acres.

Crooners, Records, and Rock and Roll

Throughout the 1940s, "swing music" of the 1930s remained the nation's favorite for dancing, whether jitterbugging or dancing close. Swing was dominated by the orchestras of Benny Goodman, Duke Ellington, and Count Basie. Each had nationally famous soloists. The most popular men were "crooners" Bing Crosby and Frank Sinatra. Singing mostly romantic songs, they stayed on top in the 1950s. New male stars such as Tony Bennett, Eddie Fisher, Harry Belafonte, and Perry Como could not displace Bing and Frank. Leading female vocalists of the 1940s—Rosemary Clooney, Peggy Lee, Ella Fitzgerald, and Sarah Vaughan—were among the most popular in the 1950s as well.

Count Basie
(Library of Congress)

The record business boomed throughout the 1940s, and the average buyers became younger each year. At first, only grownups could afford to buy records. Right through the mid-1950s, the average record buyers were in their early twenties. That changed by the close of the decade, when teenagers became the record industry's main customers. This was helped by the development of the cheaper 45 rpm record, which had a three-minute song on each side. By then, teenagers were buying more than 70 percent of all records sold. They had a new passion: rock and roll.

In 1951, radio disc jockey Alan Freed first referred to "rhythm and blues" music as "rock and roll." Before then, rhythm and blues was considered "race music" for blacks only. But by giving it a new name, Freed was able to introduce its powerful beat and catchy tunes to a broader audience. In 1955, the weekly newsmagazine *Life* published a feature on rock and roll titled: "A Frenzied Teen-Age Music Craze Kicks Up a Big Fuss."

Older folk shook their heads in disapproval at rock and roll's suggestive lyrics and sensuality. In an age when most men wore crew cuts, Elvis Presley shocked them with his ducktail haircut and loose-swinging hips. The younger generation was swept away by Presley's "Don't be Cruel" and "Hound Dog." Rock and roll became a pop-music category of its own. Black musicians like Fats Domino and Chuck Berry, who had first played this music, came into the mainstream. But frequently it was all-white rock-and-roll groups like Bill Haley and the Comets who sold the most records. Haley's "Rock Around the Clock" in 1955 sold a million copies.

Most early rock-and-roll performers were male: Buddy Holly, Little Richard, Jerry Lee Lewis, Chuck Berry, and the Everly Brothers. But they shared the record charts with female vocalists like Debbie Reynolds, Patti Page, Connie Francis, and Doris Day, who sang mostly romantic ballads. All this music came together every weekday afternoon on television's *American Bandstand*. Philadelphia host Dick Clark brought in the latest singers and local young people demonstrated the latest dances, from "The Stroll" to "The Slop." Rock and roll dominated pop music by the end of the 1950s, but it was not the only music that appealed to Americans.

Buddy Holly (LEFT); **Chuck Berry** (RIGHT) (Library of Congress)

Jazz, Folk, and Classical

In the 1940s, the music known as jazz was dividing into different categories. Swing had come out of jazz and remained broadly popular until the advent of rock and roll. Dixieland, or small-band jazz, continued in the traditions of the past: musicians playing well-known songs with lots of improvisation. As with swing, the tune always remained recognizable. Another type of jazz now developed, which had its own character. This was broadly termed "modern jazz," with one main style known as "bebop."

These new forms of jazz were not for dancing but for listening. They focused on free-form playing that featured virtuosity and originality. Among the pioneers of this type of jazz were trumpeters John "Dizzy" Gillespie and Miles Davis and saxophonist Charlie Parker. Modern jazz moved away from the mass audience, appealing more to intellectuals and sophisticates.

Interest in another American traditional music sprang up among many young people. By the end of the 1950s, folk-music groups and singers were performing old songs that had been almost forgotten. Still played in back-country homes and among the blues musicians of the South, these songs caught on with the thousands of young people who were picking up guitars and banjos themselves. For all the power of popular music of broadcast media and records, a growing number of young people wanted to play old folk tunes. This interest was inspired in part by an enduring legacy that had been kept up by folk singers such as Pete Seeger and Woody Guthrie. They interpreted old songs and wrote new ones. Many songs were biting criticisms of government and society. Seeger performed both in tiny Greenwich Village coffeehouses and before an audience of thousands in Carnegie Hall. In the 1950s, the folk audience grew rapidly, especially among the college crowd.

One of the strongest inspirations for popular interest in folk music came from an immensely popular recording by Harry Belafonte in the late 1950s. Calypso songs from his home in Jamaica became hits. Belafonte's "Day-O" and "Jamaica Farewell" opened new musical paths for young people. Around the same time, the squeaky-clean Kingston Trio appeared, giving traditional songs irresistible harmonies. The Kingston Trio made the cover of *Life* magazine in 1959. Other groups like them had an enthusiastic following.

Classical music still found an audience, though they were mainly well-educated and older. Although major orchestras that were once funded by radio stations were dying, recordings of classical music still sold steadily. Live concerts and chamber music performances were the heart and soul of the classical music world. Most of what was played and recorded had been written in the nineteenth century or earlier by Beethoven, Mozart, and Brahms. There was also a growing interest in the much earlier works of Bach and Vivaldi.

On Stage

The musical theater had some of its greatest hits in these decades. Musical romances such as *Carousel* and *Oklahoma!* reigned on Broadway through the 1940s. Each year, Broadway generated many of the nation's favorite songs, often several from the same show. Pop singers performed or recorded half a dozen hits from *Oklahoma!* in 1943.

One notable musical failure of the early 1940s was George Gershwin's *Porgy and Bess*. Set in a poor black fishing community in the South, the musical did not at first appeal to either whites or African Americans. Years later, it would become a hit Broadway show as well as a movie box-office success.

High spirits on Broadway turned to street-tough drama in 1957, with the controversial hit *West Side Story*. New York City social problems were at the heart of this portrayal of conflict between Puerto Rican and white street gangs. But other musicals were pure entertainment. In the 1950s, *Guys and Dolls*, *The King and I*, *My Fair Lady,* and *The Sound of Music* were top hits. Their stars also had successful television and film careers. They included Mary Martin, Gordon MacRae, Julie Andrews, Rex Harrison, and Yul Brynner.

Dramatic plays continued to be popular. During the war, Broadway audiences flocked to *Harvey,* by Mary Chase. In this comedy, a well-to-do but eccentric man becomes acquainted with a large rabbit invisible to most other people. Jimmy Stewart later starred in the movie version, which also was a hit.

Two of the nation's most talented playwrights, Tennessee Williams and Arthur Miller, were making their mark on serious theater. Williams's *The Glass Menagerie* and Miller's *Death of a*

Books Keep on Selling

The arrival of television worried many publishers and writers who feared that books would lose their popular appeal. Yet book sales dramatically increased by more than 50 percent during the 1950s. In 1958, more than 350 million books were sold. One reason for the leap in sales was the paperback. Instead of paying for an expensive hardcover, readers could pick up paperbacks for as little as twenty-five cents. Most readers bought two or three paperbacks at a time and read them quickly. Eventually even the greatest literature would find its way to paperback, to be read by more people than ever.

At least one publisher thanked television for book-selling success. He said more people were staying home in the evenings to watch television. By the time their favorite shows were over, they were too tired to go out. So they read books before they went to sleep.

The book world was dominated, as ever, by the novel. Ernest Hemingway and John Steinbeck were the top fiction authors for much of these decades. Hemingway had become a media personality by the late 1950s. *Life* magazine had him on its cover at least twice in this decade, a sure sign of stardom. As in every generation, romantic novels were the overall best-selling category. *Peyton Place* by Grace Metalious was so successful that it became a popular television drama. Almost as popular as romances were detective mysteries. One of the top-selling authors in this category was Mickey Spillane, who created hard-boiled detective Mike Hammer. Fans bought 27 million novels, most in paperback, featuring Spillane's "private-eye" hero.

Salesman had long runs after World War II ended.

Into the 1950s, the war continued to influence the theater. The drama *The Caine Mutiny Court Martial* from Herman Wouk's novel of the same title and the comedy *No Time for Sergeants* by Ira Levin recalled military service. *The Diary of Anne Frank* (1955) told the inspiring but tragic true story of a doomed Jewish girl in Nazi Europe. Also in the 1950s, Miller's *The Crucible* used the Salem witch trials as a parable for the Army-McCarthy hearings.

Amateur theatrics were popular as well. Thornton Wilder's much-loved *Our Town* from 1938 was performed so often that on almost any given day it could be seen somewhere in the United States. Americans could recognize themselves in its moving story of a small town and its inhabitants.

Ted Williams
(Library of Congress)

Sports—Watching and Playing

For boys and men, the main participation sports were baseball (stickball in cities) and football (usually touch football on playgrounds). Also, boxing was part of almost every young man's life. Almost every town of any size had rings for regular boxing matches. These rings often were in sports "gardens," or arenas that could hold hundreds or even thousands of fans. There would be matches every Friday night, in several weight classes, from lightest to heaviest. The heavyweights were the stars of the show and fought last.

All over the country there were boxing gyms. Young men trained with dreams of making it to the greatest boxing venue of all: New York's Madison Square Garden. Amateur fighters entered tournaments sponsored by the Golden Gloves or the Amateur Athletic Union. Local tournament winners went on to regional and then to national championships. If they had ability, they could be signed by a professional trainer who would try to make a pro out of them.

In this era, boxers were widely admired. The ideal athlete was the professional boxer who was courageous, talented, and modest. In the 1940s, an African American named Joe Louis was the reigning world champion until retiring in 1949.

In the mid-1950s, the most admired boxer was heavyweight champion Rocky Marciano. After an undefeated career, Marciano retired as undisputed heavyweight champion in 1956.

Baseball was the national pastime. Even during World War II, when the best professionals were in the service, the pro game went on. One of the most remarkable war-era players was Pete Grey, a one-armed center fielder for the St. Louis Browns. Baseball made a special rule for Grey: after catching the ball, he could drop his glove to make a throw.

Some 545 women played as part of the All-American Girls Professional League, beginning in 1943. Started by Chicago Cubs owner Philip Wrigley, the women drew a million fans by 1948.

But the league folded in 1954, largely as a result of competition from televised men's professional baseball.

The greatest team of the era was the New York Yankees. The wealthy Yankees could acquire the best players of the day. Other clubs from smaller cities could not match the Yankee treasury, and so could not field such star-studded teams. In these decades, the Yankees dominated the American League and won the World Series ten times.

The leading players of these decades included Joe DiMaggio and Mickey Mantle of the Yankees, Jackie Robinson of the Brooklyn Dodgers, and Ted Williams of the Boston Red Sox. Willie Mays of the New York Giants and Henry Aaron of the Milwaukee Braves had joined the top ranks by the mid-1950s. All

Althea Gibson
(Library of Congress)

were great hitters. Robinson also had to his credit the breaking of the "color line"—integrating professional baseball. Robinson defied racism and at the same time won the National League batting championship in 1949.

In the 1940s, football was mainly a college sport. Professional football did not yet offer the excitement or fan loyalty of the "rah-rah" college game. The top college teams of the era were Southern California, Oklahoma, California, Michigan State, Ohio State, Notre Dame, Army, and U.C.L.A. The National Football League's dominant teams were the New York Giants, Washington Redskins, Chicago Bears, and Cleveland Browns. The Browns had perhaps the finest running back of all time in Jim Brown. In 1958, only his second pro year, Brown set a single-season NFL record for rushing, with 1,527 yards.

Basketball was a minor sport through most of this period. National college championships had been established in 1939, and the first professional championships were held in 1947. The professional Basketball Association of America changed its name in 1949 to the National Basketball Association (NBA). In the 1950s, gyms were small, crowds were small, and salaries were small. The sport's best clubs often were in cities such as Rochester, Indianapolis, and Fort Wayne, Indiana. The New York Knickerbockers and Minneapolis Lakers dominated the 1950s until the Boston Celtics became the team to beat by the close of the decade.

In 1955, *Life* magazine featured high-school phenomenon Wilt "The Stilt" Chamberlain. Already seven feet tall at age eighteen, Chamberlain joined the Philadelphia Warriors. He was the NBA scoring champion from 1960 to 1966. By then, basketball was firmly established as one of the most exciting sports in the United States.

Other Games and Sports

In the 1940s and 1950s, thoroughbred horse racing was one of the most popular spectator sports. The Kentucky Derby in the spring was the crowning event of each racing season. Whirlaway and Citation were the betting favorites in the 1940s, as each achieved racing's highest triumph, the Triple Crown. This honor comes from winning three key races in a season: the Kentucky Derby, the Preakness Stakes, and the Belmont Stakes. The finest horses of the season are entered into these races in pursuit of the Triple Crown. Whirlaway won all three and became the Triple Crown winner in 1941. Citation did the same in 1948.

Professional tennis had a few well-known stars, led by Jack Kramer in the mid-1940s. Women's tennis offered one of the most notable events of the period: Althea Gibson won the national singles championship in the 1957–1958 season. Gibson was the first African American to rise to the top in American tennis. By the close of the 1950s, a youth boom erupted to make tennis a widely popular sport, and new tennis courts had been built at suburban high schools.

Professional golf had stars in Sam Snead and Ben Hogan, who dominated much of this period. At the end of the 1950s, they were overtaken by Arnold Palmer, who would become one of the most popular athletes in the country by the early 1960s. Golf was rising in popularity. Televised tournaments attracted millions of fans, and new golf courses were being built in the suburbs. The nine-hole "pitch and putt" game also brought new interest. Pitch and putt became a popular pastime for young people on a date. Golf was prepared for a meteoric rise in the next decade.

Bowling alleys were also opening up in the suburbs, most found in newly built strip malls. Alleys attracted a younger generation of participants who bowled in local leagues. As with other sports, the best bowlers could compete professionally.

Soccer was popular with immigrant communities, mainly in cities and also in prep schools and college. By the end of the 1950s, the sport was beginning to gain a solid youth following. Many high schools established teams as a cheaper alternative to football. By 1960, there were as many colleges playing soccer as played football, and high-school participation was climbing. Girls and women were not yet playing soccer, but new youth soccer clubs and leagues were being formed all around the country.

The United States was enjoying greater prosperity than ever before. Americans had more opportunity to savor their leisure— and more forms of entertainment to explore. As the 1960s unfolded, two phenomena of this era—rock and roll and television—would become even more dominant. Others, like radio and serious theater, would decline. Throughout it all, the call of "Play ball!" would continue to resound across the land.

Chapter Nine

Fashions and Fads

The film *Rebel Without a Cause* (LEFT), and especially its star, actor James Dean, were very popular with young audiences. Many teens identified with the hero's rejection of older generation's values. One popular toy craze of the 1950s was the Hula Hoop. As the photograph (RIGHT) illustrates, it was popular with people in almost all walks of life. (Library of Congress)

World War II caused drastic shortages of new clothing. Even so, there were always new trends in fashion, such as clever patchwork or military-style tailoring. After the war, tastes in fashion told much about the wearer's personality and even his or her politics. The traditional wear of the middle class was rejected by young rebels of the 1950s.

Yet, high fashion remained at the heart of American culture and tradition. In 1960, *Life* magazine published a retrospective of the years since its founding in 1936. A feature on women's fashions was titled "The Golden Days of Style." The editors wrote: "What women wore was more varied than ever, but through all the changes, the glamor of fashion proved enduring."

Just as enduring was the influence of film stars and celebrities. From movie heroines to queens, crooners to athletes, celebrities set the example for the nation to follow. Another enduring influence on American life was the "jitterbug," which kept the nation dancing from the 1930s to the 1950s.

In the 1950s, as baby boomers came of age, movies began to cater to them. Horror movies in 3-D, movies about rebellious young people, and movies featuring rock and roll were cranked out in quick succession.

The 1950s brought some fads that are still connected in the public mind with that era—the Hula Hoop, crowding into phone booths or a Volkswagon Beetle, Bermuda shorts, and ducktail haircuts. More seriously, its experiments with abstract expressionism in painting, attractions to flying saucers, and to anti-heroes and "beatniks" signalled the social restlessness of the decades to come.

Men's Fashions Trim Down

The men's baggy "zoot suit" of the 1930s was still popular in the early 1940s. The zoot suit had wide trousers that narrowed at the cuffs, and a long, draped coat. The need for cloth for the military limited what was available for civilian production. After the war began, the zoot suit gave way to clothes that required less material.

Men's wear became more conservative and remained that way after the war. Gray flannel suits became standard for businesmen and college students. Lapels were widened or trimmed from year to year. The wide ties of the 1940s gave way to narrow ones in the 1950s. A starched white shirt was preferred for most of the era, but in the 1950s, pink became a daring color choice.

Casual wear might include a plaid shirt, sports jacket or pants. President Truman was noted for the flowered Hawaiian shirts he wore on Florida vacations after the war, and other men wore them too.

By the end of the 1950s, Americans had tired of proper, uncomfortable clothing. Out of the office, the jacket gave way to the sweater, and some men turned to khakis or the jeans of their childhood. Men also began to wear Bermuda shorts as casual attire. Although men in other countries had worn shorts, American men rarely did until then. Older men wore them with knee-length socks and leather shoes. Young men generally wore them with ankle socks and sneakers or loafers with no socks at all. Or they might wear tennis shoes, which were becoming fashionable off the court.

Saddle shoes worn with bobby sox remained popular among young people. Introduced in the 1930s, they endured the 1940s and early 1950s, but in the late 1950s, many wanted white bucks like crooner Pat Boone or blue suede shoes like Elvis Presley.

Through most of the period, men's hair was cut short. After the war, the "flat top" and the "crew cut" were popular. Men often topped them with a fedora in the winter and a straw hat in the summer. With the coming of rock and roll, many younger men let their hair grow longer, in defiance of the older generation. In the coming decades, it would be much longer.

A few young trendsetters responded to the beatnik influence in the late 1950s. They adopted black turtle necks and baggy sweaters, grew beards, and wore their hair short under a beret.

Women's Wartime Fashions

Few clothing shops had much new to sell during the war. Regulations required clothing to use as little material as possible. Hems, for example, could be no more than two inches. Blouses could have only one pocket. No hoods or shawls were allowed on dresses, and there were no cuffs on coats. Such limitations led to the "convertible suit" for women. This was a jacket, short skirt, and blouse. The jacket was worn to work, but it could be cast off for a dressier look in the evening. Women showed their legs more than ever. Because of war shortages, however, stockings were hard to get. Some women drew a seam down the back of their legs so it appeared they were wearing stockings.

Skimpy, two-piece bathing suits first came out in 1944. They were scandalous to many people. Yet, two-piece bathing suits did save on fabric, in keeping with the conservation of the war years.

The two-piece convertible suit of the 1940s
(Dover Publications)

Old clothes were repaired to last longer. Home seamstresses took pride in sewing imaginative patches on clothes. In 1943, the mode became women's sweaters for all occasions. Also in style were "his and her" bow ties.

In time, there was plenty of surplus military clothing for sale. This gear was sold for leisure sports. Women's short-legged military overalls were bestsellers. Toward the end of the war, in 1945, new women's fashions began to take on a military look. Teenage girls might wear "I.D.," bracelets with their names (and sometimes their boyfriend's too), and hung dog chains around their waists.

Freedom and Fashion

During four years of war, working women became used to having more personal freedom. Many wore slacks and overalls to work in the factories. Until then, pants were considered unfeminine, even improper.

In wartime, increasingly more women wore makeup. Prior to this, makeup was thought to be garish. The "painted lady" was suspected as being immoral. Makeup now became socially acceptable, and red lipstick and nail polish were the rage. High-heel shoes replaced sensible ones. Women's new styles and their newfound independence went together.

When it came to more formal attire, proper ladies wore hats Hatmaking was big business. At gatherings of women there would be all sorts of hats: flowered, wide-brimmed, narrow-brimmed, hats worn high on the head, over the brow, or at an angle. Hats were lacquered, some made of straw, others of leather or fur. Some had colorful hat bands, others were without bands—but they almost always had artificial flowers, especially silk ones.

After the war, French designer Christian Dior soon set the keynote for women's clothing. His designs were elegant and luxurious. Skirts were long and full, with tight waists, the shoulders and bosoms full and round. Fashion editors at the magazines *Glamour*, *Harper's Bazaar*, and *Vogue* oozed with admiration for Dior's "New Look" from Paris in 1947. Patches, military cuts, sweaters, blouses, and short skirts were out. Legs were to be covered. Dior's style sold to the fashionable and wealthy, but many women refused to go along with it. They even signed angry petitions against Dior's fashions. After years of wartime independence, American women were not eager to be dressed up like frilly dolls.

A More Casual Look

Raccoon coats were briefly back in vogue in 1948, as they had been 30 years earlier. That same year, loose-fitting Hawaiian muumuus were favored by many women. Muumuus would remain popular through the 1950s. The first bikini bathing suits appeared too. Bikinis were two-piece bathing suits, but even had even less material than the two-piece suits that came out during the war. They were named for a tiny island in the Pacific where nuclear weapons were tested.

During the war, short haircuts had been very popular. Later, hair was often curled high on the head in front and worn long to the shoulders in back. The 1950s brought many new hairstyles. One of the most appealing was the ponytail in which the hair was pulled back and gathered with elastic or a clip into a single cascade. It first appeared around 1952.

Among young women, short kilts and circular felt skirts with poodles appliqued on them became popular. The sweater was now a favorite and common article of clothing. It was worn singly or in matching sets. Sack dresses, which fell straight from the shoulder, were re-introduced in 1957. They had been popular among factory workers early in the century.

Clothing by a new designer caught the new spirit of many young well-to-do women. American Bill Blass had an original style, classic, yet elegant. His designs won many awards and even included tailored blue jeans. Until then, jeans had not been high fashion.

Like men, women began to dress casually for informal occasions. They wore slacks, Bermuda shorts, and short-shorts instead of dresses, although not to work or religious services. They often wore tennis shoes, sandals, or "flats" rather than shoes with heels—high or low.

Idols to Imitate

Many Americans took their cues about how to dress and wear their hair from news and movie magazines. Magazines highlighted the most beautiful and interesting women of the day. The long, blond coiffure of actress Veronica Lake got three full pages in *Life*. The editors were so impressed that they described her hair as "a property of world influence." Lake was one of the most popular actresses during the war, but the government asked the studios to pull her hair back. Many female workers were imitating her hairstyle that covered one eye, and their hair was getting caught in machinery.

During the war, "pin-up" photos of stars like Rita Hayworth, Janet Blair, and Betty Grable were popular with servicemen at their posts around the world. Hayworth and Blair popularized the form-fitting sweater, and Grable's legs, exposed by a bathing suit, became famous.

Not all the icons were movie stars. First Lady Mamie

Eisenhower with her blue eyes and bangs was a model of post war femininity. A seasoned military wife, she restored a festive atmosphere to the White House that had been curtailed by the Great Depression and World War II. (The White House was renovated during the Truman administration.) Mamie Eisenhower also doted on her grandchildren and shared her fudge recipe with the public.

Mamie Eisenhower
(Library of Congress)

Also in the 1950s limelight was actress Grace Kelly. Known for her icy beauty, Kelly starred in movies by Alfred Hitchcock that included *Dial M for Murder* and *Rear Window*. In 1954, she won an Oscar for her performance against type as the embittered wife of an alcoholic in *Country Girl*. Then, she became a princess by marrying the prince of Monaco, a small kingdom in Europe on the Mediterranean. It was every fan's fantasy come true.

Americans were fascinated with royalty. They also admired Elizabeth II of Great Britain. First as a princess and then as queen, Elizabeth was in several *Life* features and on the cover.

Among men, actors were also trendsetters. The 1940s offered both the polished and the rough-hewn. The cosmopolitan Clark Gable and Erroll Flynn, with their pencil-thin mustaches and dark good looks were one kind of model. Jimmy Stewart and Gary Cooper wore buckskins and cowboy hats to go with their rugged masculinity. The charming Fred Astaire was the suave prince of high society. Then there were the city tough guys. They included the tough-talking Humphrey Bogart, waving a cigarette cupped in one hand, and James Cagney, quick on his feet and with his fists.

Gary Cooper
(Library of Congress)

Bandleaders Duke Ellington and Cab Calloway were role models for African American men. Both were always elegantly dressed in front of their jazz musicians. Pop star celebrities of the 1950s became widely imitated, too. Rock and rollers Elvis Presley and Fabian persuaded many young men to comb their own hair into "ducktails."

One Hollywood personality combined the attributes of a real-life hero and an accomplished actor. The boyish good looks of Audie Murphy revealed nothing of his military accomplishments. Murphy was the most decorated American soldier of World War II. He won the Medal of Honor and France's Croix de Guerre, along with many other medals for valor. He wrote a book about his wartime experiences called *To Hell and Back* in 1949. In 1955, it was made into a movie with him as its star. The movie set a record for gross revenues that was not broken until *Jaws* was released in the 1970s. The concept of "hero" was beginning to come into question, however.

A Younger Audience

Handsome and moody actors—first Marlon Brando, then James Dean—became admired by many, especially young people. Their "anti-hero" characters were flawed, like ordinary men. Yet, the anti-hero showed courage in adversity. He was more realistic than the idealized heroes of film and television. He struggled in the real world and rejected the make-believe of show business.

Brando's *The Wild One* about a motorcycle gang in 1953, and Dean's *East of Eden* (from a John Steinbeck novel about two brothers) and *Rebel Without a Cause*, both released in 1955, stirred young people with their expressions of youthful anger. In *Rebel*, Dean drove a custom 1949 Mercury, stripped of all its chrome, which appealed greatly to teens. Not long after, he died while making his third movie, *Giant*. Dean was killed when his Porsche sports car crashed.

Not all movies made for teens were as well-acted as those with Brando and Dean. In 1952, Hollywood produced movies in two new processes designed to compete with television. Cinerama was shot with three cameras and had to be projected from three points onto extra-wide screens. Special effects that brought the viewer along on experiences like a roller coaster ride were a part of *This is Cinerama*. Another process, developed by Polaroid, allowed viewers to experience a movie in three dimension. In order to view 3-D movies, the viewer wore special glasses. Movies like *Bwana Devil* and *Creature from the Black Lagoon* were famous for the screams they produced from theater audiences. Other movies were made in 3-D, but the fad never entered the mainstream.

Instead, studios turned out a stream of movies like *Blackboard Jungle*, *Crime in the Streets*, and *Cry Baby Killer* dealing with wayward "juvenile delinquents." There were even movies about tough girls: *Girls in the Night* and *Girl Gang*, for example. Sandra Dee starred in *The Restless Years* with John Saxon as her boyfriend from the wrong side of the tracks. Then there

Moviegoers watch the movie *Bwana Devil* with 3-D glasses. (CORBIS)

were movies made to showcase rock and roll acts. *Rock Around the Clock*, with disc jockey Alan Freed and Bill Haley and the Comets was followed by *Rock, Rock, Rock, Shake, Rattle and Roll, Don't Knock the Rock, The Big Beat*, and many more.

By the end of the 1950s, the genres began to merge in B grade films like *Teenage Caveman, Teenage Monster, Teenage Zombies*, and *Teenagers from Outer Space*.

Games and Dances

In the 1940s, many favorite games and fads of the 1930s remained popular. Some spread even more widely across the country in the next decades. For example, Bingo, started in 1938, kept going strong. So did "slumber parties," which became a must for young girls. Girls often brought attention to themselves by wearing sleighbells on their socks.

Every year there was always a new crop of "knock-knock" jokes, which had started in the mid-1930s. Another trend was taking candid photography instead of formal, posed shots.

In spite of television's growth, home entertainment still focused around games of all sorts. In 1949, the card game Canasta first appeared. A few years later, in 1952, families were playing the immensely popular new word game, Scrabble.

Another holdover from the 1930s was dancing the jitterbug,

popular since 1936. Through the wartime era, "Jitterbug Jamborees" appealed to millions of young Americans. On any weekend evening, they would be dancing various versions of the jitterbug. It might be the "Lindy Hop" in Midwestern American Legion halls or the "Big Apple" at Webster Hall in Greenwich Village, New York. There were after-work parties at factories, where co-workers got together to dance. Parties at the giant Lockheed company's aircraft plants were jokingly called the "Swing Shift." This term referred both to an eight-hour work shift as well as to the "swing" music played for dancing.

Jitterbugging often involved remarkable athleticism. Dancers kept up a frenetic pace. The woman would leap over her partner's head or roll across his back. The joy of the music and dancing was almost more important than who the partner was.

By 1954, the jitterbug was being challenged by the Cuban mambo and the cha-cha-cha. But the jitterbug managed to adapt to the new beat of rock and roll a few years later. Other dancers joined a line to dance the bouncy "bunny hop."

Kids' Stuff

Toys related to film characters became big business in this era. Walt Disney films set the pace, with many animated film characters that appealed to children. Snow White, Cinderella, and the Seven Dwarves were favorites, along with Mickey Mouse and Donald Duck. In 1942, the animated film, *Bambi*, introduced the adorable fawn with the big eyes. Bambi won the hearts of children everywhere, and appealed to their parents as well.

In 1955, Disney's enormously popular adventure film *Davy Crockett* stimulated a craze for coonskin caps. The main competition for coonskin was the cowboy hat. The most famous cowboy and cowgal were singing stars Roy Rogers and his wife Dale Evans. Children wanted to be like Roy and Dale, dressed in cowboy outfits with two-gun holsters.

Cartoon characters from the comic strips also had a youthful following. One was Li'l Abner, the handsome hillbilly bumpkin from Dogpatch, U.S.A. Li'l Abner dolls became popular in the 1950s, as did yo-yos, Silly Putty, trampolines, and Slinky toys. None, however, compared in popularity with the hula hoop craze of 1958. This plastic hoop was put around the waist. Then the wearer did a clumsy version of the Hawaiian dance, the hula. The idea was to keep the hoop going for as long as possible. Experts could hula many hoops at one time. The hoop was also whirled around arms, legs, and even the neck. Sometimes hoops were going simultaneously on all those places. Hula Hoops were a colossal, but short-lived fad.

In 1959, a toy appeared that would endure for generations: the Barbie Doll. Barbie was a tall blonde with an endless wardrobe. In the decades to come, she would be a mainstay of girls' toys.

Of all the activities of American youngsters, talking on the telephone was perhaps the favorite. In 1956, *Life* magazine ran a feature titled, "Tireless, Talky Teenagers and Toiling Telephones." At a time when only a rare home had more than one telephone line, teenagers' use of the family phone was a source of constant complaint.

College students pile into a phone booth.
(Library of Congress)

Flying Saucers

In 1947, a pilot over Washington State described nine "saucerlike things" that zoomed past at more than 1,000 mph. This was the start of the "flying saucer craze." Many more such sightings and reports followed, from all across the country. By the mid-1950s, more than 600 sightings were reported every year. College students, farmers, and lawmen all claimed to have seen "unidentified flying objects," or UFOs.

The air force started a massive investigation to find out what people were actually seeing. No conclusive answer was ever reached. Some thought the air force itself was actually behind many of the sightings. They believed these "space ships" were actually experimental military aircraft being secretly tested. The flying saucer craze did not fade throughout this era, and people kept reporting UFOs. Many people hoped to see a flying saucer, and scanned the skies at night. Some enthusiasts carried cameras everywhere they went. They hoped to be the next lucky photographer to snap a UFO photo and sell it to the media.

College Fads

Through the 1950s, "college men" and "coeds" became important trendsetters. This was especially so in fads, such as wearing small hats called "beanies." Goldfish-eating contests and stuffing a record number of people into phone booths or Volkswagens were attention-getting college events.

Celebrating Sadie Hawkins Day was becoming a tradition in colleges and high schools. Sadie Hawkins was a character in the comic strip "Li'l Abner." She was always trying to marry Li'l Abner, but he always refused her. On Sadie Hawkins Day, females pursued males, usually by inviting them on dates. At a time when strict sex roles dictated that men always initiated relationships with women, this was remarkable.

In the early 1950s, pizza became the most popular fast food, and "pizza parlors" sprang up everywhere. They were the favorite meeting place for young people after a movie or a dance.

By 1959, college undergrads were "hunkerin'." This meant almost sitting on the floor—squatting—as they socialized. Until now, adults sitting on the floor was unusual and not proper. Hunkerin' was a phase before a general trend of the 1960s. Then, sitting together on the floor became normal, even preferred, for young people.

Art: From Pollock to Rockwell

Modernists who fled Nazi persecution in Europe had a powerful influence on American art in this era. These painters, sculptors, and photographers came to the United States after the war. They brought a radical way of looking at the world, and their art reflected it. Many artists, including the "abstract expressionists," declared the only true art was "art for art's sake." In other words, the act of creating art was more important than any message behind the art. Modernists opposed "representational art" that showed actual things, places, or people. They called for abstraction instead of "sentimental" pictures.

Willem de Kooning
(Library of Congress)

The leading American artist of the modernist movement was abstract expressionist Jackson Pollock. His wild, unruly "spatter paintings" earned him high fees in the mid-1950s. Pollock said painting is first and foremost "a state of self-discovery" for the artist. Another modernist was Mark Rothko, whose massive, painted blocks of color startled and overwhelmed viewers. Others included Willem de Kooning, Robert Motherwell, and Piet Mondrian. Most moved on from abstract expressionism to other styles, but all were committed to artistic freedom. Many developed fresh new ideas. Sculptor Alexander Calder created mobiles that employed motion. His sculptures were created from "found objects" and steel rather than being carved from marble or cast in bronze.

While the modernists opened new and unpredictable avenues, traditional painters continued to work successfully. These had a much larger public following. Through this period, weekly magazines like *The Saturday Evening Post* reached millions of readers. *The Post* used artists to illustrate their stories and for their eye-catching covers. Illustrator Norman Rockwell was the leading "cover artist" for the *Post* and other top publications. Rockwell's pictures of hometown life, usually humorous, touched Americans everywhere.

Thousands of Americans rushed to keep up with the latest art craze or visited museums to view classical art. But millions more turned to much-loved illustrators like Norman Rockwell for their artistic enjoyment.

The Beat Generation

Beatniks appeared in the 1950s as a reaction to the culture of conformity and like-thinking. They rebelled against accepted morals and what they considered the hypocrisy of mainstream America. Beats loved jazz and folk music, which they shared with their friends in small, intimate coffeehouses. Their poets, Lawrence Ferlinghetti and Allen Ginsberg, recited verse to the accompaniment of jazz or guitar-strumming or bongo drums.

Jive Talk

"Hey, Daddy-O, that's cool!" was an exclamation of approval by the "hipsters," or "cool cats," of this era. Slang terms were shared by the Beats, the street gangs, jazz musicians, and teenagers. This was termed "jive talk," meaning a language known mainly to insiders. "Jive" came from the early jazz scene in New Orleans. One general meaning then was phony talk, or lies.

Each social or cultural group had its own pet language. Gang members in cities called a large-scale fight a "rumble." Girls and young women were often called "chicks." Most people thought this word had to do with "cute as a chick." In fact, the much older New Orleans jazz term for young women was the French term "chic," meaning stylish.

Jazz influenced most of the slang: "cool," for commendable or outstanding; "swinging," for good music with rhythm; "with it," for being aware of what was going on; "the most," for the best; "pad," for home; "cat," for a man, or someone who's "hip," which means "with it." Slang terms that became popular in the 1940s included "groovy," "far out," "crazy," "dig," "flip," "hang loose," "a drag," and "square." They were still in use at the century's end.

Slang differed, depending on who was speaking: hot-rodders racing one another, city toughs, middle-class high schoolers, and the military. Even space scientists had their own slang: a "bird" was a rocket, or missile; "snakebite," was an accident; an "Egads Button," was pushed to blow up a missile or rocket that had gone off course. "Egads" was an ancient exclamation meaning "Oh no!" The Beatniks first popularized the use of "like" as a "pause word"—instead of "um." This usage of "like" faded away for a while. It was destined to be revived by a new generation of young people, forty years later.

Beatnik culture was more than a passing fad for most of them. It was part of a new way of thinking that harked back to European radicals of centuries before. Those earlier rebels had been termed Bohemians. Beats assumed that same label. They had a language all their own.

They were "beat" because society had broken them down. They claimed no ambition for social success. The "nik" came from a Russian suffix comparable to "er," as in "fighter" or "driver." Male beatniks typically wore sloppy clothes, sweaters, and sandals. Their hair was cropped short, and they often had beards. Females favored black leotards, turtleneck tops and heavy eyeshadow that often gave them "raccoon eyes."

Jack Kerouac's novel *On the Road*, published in 1957, became the signature fiction of the Beat life. It was a thinly disguised autobiographical account of a young man, Sal Paradise, and his trip across the country with a friend. Poetic and raw, the narrative imitated jazz and became a sensation. The book continued to sell handsomely throughout the century.

Young people who were not truly Beats still came under the influence of this anti-establishment subculture. As America became more prosperous and more conservative, many teens longed for something more exciting than suburbia. Never having experienced poverty or war, they rejected the materialism and middle-class ideals of their parents. Some of their restlessness had no direction. They did not know what to do with it. In time, the civil rights and anti-war movements would become the cause so many young rebels were after.

Toward the 1960s

Between 1941 and 1960 American society had moved from relative poverty to enormous prosperity. It had entered a second world war in which it had emerged victorious as of the world's great powers. But it had given birth to a generation that no first-hand experience with either poverty or war. Despite the threat of the Cold War with the Soviet Union, Americans were more at ease in the world than ever. Whatever the changing tastes from year to year, they were moving toward a more casual lifestyle. That new lifestyle would reach full development in the decades to come. And more and more Americans would determine the fads and fashions that spread around the world.

Bibliography

Ahearn, Robert. *Decades of Cold War: American Heritage Illustrated History of the United States, Volume 16*. New York: Choice Publishing, 1988.

Bowen, Ezra, ed. *This Fabulous Century: Volume III 1940–1950*. New York: Time-Life Books, 1991.

——————. *This Fabulous Century: Volume IV 1950–1960*. New York: Time-Life Books, 1991.

Ciment, James. *The Young People's History of the United States*. New York: Barnes and Noble Books, 1998.

Derks, Scott. *Working Americans, 1880–1999*. Lakeville, CT: Greyhouse Publishing, 2000.

Green, Harvey. *The Uncertainty of Everyday Life, 1915-1945*. New York: HarperCollins Publishers, Inc., 1992.

Groner, Alex. *The History of American Business and Industry*. New York: American Heritage, 1972.

Harvey, Edmund H. *Our Glorious Century*. Pleasantville, NY: Reader's Digest Association, 2000.

Mintz, Steven and Susan Kellogg. *Domestic Revolutions: A Social History of American Family Life*. New York: The Free Press, 1988.

Index

Note: Page numbers in *italics* refer to illustrations.